The Success of Failure

A self-help guide to convert failures into success

Bhushan Kachru

Published by:

F-2/16, Ansari Road, Daryaganj, New Delhi-110002
☎ 011-23240026, 011-23240027 • *Fax:* 011-23240028
Email: info@vspublishers.com • *Website:* www.vspublishers.com

Regional Office : Hyderabad
5-1-707/1, Brij Bhawan (Beside Central Bank of India Lane)
Bank Street, Koti, Hyderabad - 500 095
☎ 040-24737290
E-mail: vspublishershyd@gmail.com

Branch Office Mumbai
Jaywant Industrial Estate, 1st Floor–108, Tardeo Road
Opposite Sobo Central, Mumbai - 400 034
☎ 022-23510736
E-mail: vspublishersmum@gmail.com

Follow us on:   

All books available at **www.vspublishers.com**

ISBN 978-93-815887-4-1
Edition: 2019

Printed at Param Offseters Okhla New Delhi-110020

Publisher's Note

V&S Publishers has come up with a number of books on Personality Development and Self –Enhancement, a type of motivation that works to make people feel good about themselves and to maintain one's self-esteem. ***The Success of Failure*** is also one among these exclusive self-motivational and self-development books written by an eminent and veteran writer, Prof. Bhushan Kachru, who has an illustrious career of over four decades in Human Resource and Development, Corporate Training, Motivational Coaching and Counselling, Personal Growth and Development, etc.

The book provides a complete and in-depth insight into a person's mental state, who has failed once or twice to achieve his/her goal or target in life and feels dejected and disappointed. According to the author, these failures should inspire the person to fuel power within himself/herself and generate the drive and passion to stay focussed amidst all such disappointments.

This book basically inspires us to convert all our failures into success and learn how to imbibe the 'can do attitude' to create new directions to speed up our success campaign.

Therefore, it is a 'must read' for all those who feel that they are at a crossroad in their personal or professional lives due to personal or professional failures and want to begin their success campaign all over again with new vigour and enthusiasm.

In the loving memory of
my respected parents
Amar Nath Kachru and
Satyawati Kachru

Foreword

Failure is a temporary stopover en route to one's cherished desire of accomplishing success. It is an opportunity to seize a lost dream and to refurbish self before recommencing journey to usher in a new dawn with new hope and vigour. The subject of failure is rarely touched upon because generally, people believe that this is a dreaded word, negative sign and bad prophecy. Surprisingly, most forget that 'Failure is the mother of Success' and that one can change and succeed with the power of failure.

This book is a road map to move beyond personal failures and disappointments and is full of practical suggestions, tips and techniques. I feel it will be an eye-opener and useful for students, business executives, engineers, professionals, entrepreneurs and those who are absorbed in tracking down their success goals. Failure is a passing phase of life that may leave one feeling helpless, unhappy, alienated and low on feelings. But no one irrespective of positions, levels, might or richness has shadowed away from it. In fact, their failures became a pedestal and pledge to conquer success.

Failure is often a Guru that teaches what otherwise one would not learn. It gives a sense of direction and chance to reassess self, mistakes and execute a well thought out plan to bounce back and be in reckoning. Failure is never final, just like success. So run, knock, stumble, bend, jump and dash to your goals so that you are unstoppable and cruise your way to success.

To overcome failures, start with small goals and practise to build the habit of achieving success by unlocking the faculties of mind and giving fear, disappointments, difficulties a permanent go by in a planned way. On using the guidelines given in the book successfully, there would be incremental gains and positive results are bound to ensue gradually. Remember, there is no ready-made formula to accomplish success except assess and change your actions, behaviour, be focussed and patiently work hard on your objective. In order to follow your dreams, it is all about what you are prepared to sacrifice and what move really inspires you.

I take this opportunity to welcome Prof. Bhushan Kachru's initiative, enthusiasm and efforts in writing this simple, empowering and motivating self-help book containing practical and realistic guidelines. I am confident the book will generate much needed interest and mental comfort for all those who fail in their success pursuits and feel that they are at a crossroad in their professional life. It will surely stimulate, arouse and activate their resilience to fight it out and turn tables on failures.

25th July, 2012

Dr. H. Chaturvedi
Director
Birla Institute of Management Technology (BIMTECH)
Greater Noida (NCR) UP-201306

Don't Quit

When things go wrong, as they sometimes will,
When the road you're trudging seems all uphill,
When the funds are low and the debts are high
And you want to smile, but you have to sigh,
When care is pressing you down a bit,
Rest, If you must, but do not quit.
Life is queer with its twists and turns
As every one of us sometimes learns
And many a failure turns about
When he might have won, had he stuck it out;
Don't give up though the pace seems slow
You may succeed with another blow.
Success is failure turned inside out –
The silver tint of the clouds of doubt,
And you never can tell how close you are,
It may be near when it seems so far;
So stick to the fight when you're hardest hit –
It's when things seem worst that you mustn't quit.

—*Anonymous*

Acknowledgements

This book has been written with the help and encouragement of many and I am deeply indebted to all of them. However, it is a special pleasure to acknowledge the contributions of the following:

I am obliged to various authors, great philosophers and thinkers for having used their astounding, useful and pertinent quotes, references and sayings which has made the book captivating. But for these, the objectives of the book would have been incomplete. These quotes will go a long way in inspiring and arousing the readers to fight out their failures with zeal and give a new lease of life to their endeavors.

I am grateful for the encouragement and blessings received from my elders, Mr. P. N. Dhar and Mrs. Veena Dhar. I offer special thanks for their help and inspiration. I am thankful to Dr. H. Chaturvedi, Director, Birla Institute of Management Technology (BIMTECH) for agreeing to write foreword to the book.

I am appreciative of my consort, Rita Kachru for her love, support and help in supplementing the book with various practical examples from day to day life and also feeding me with nutritious food to remain agile. It was magnanimous of her to hold my hand in moments of extreme gloominess and despair. If it wasn't for her, I would have never realised that there is 'Success hidden in every Failure'.

I am proud of my children who at each stage stood behind me like a solid rock and kept driving me to march ahead:

(Daughter) Barkha Dhar, a budding published writer and blogger (dharbarkha.blogspot.com) based in USA for providing her invaluable insight and out of the box quotes and a beautiful and crisp couplet on mind. I highly appreciate her efforts in going through some parts of the manuscript and giving her valuable and intellectual inputs.

Son Aditya Kachru, for his innovative and creative communication inputs, valued contributions in designing a creative and inspired book cover. His timeless contributions on many facets of failure-success saga and continued prop up are highly appreciative.

(Son-in-law) Nitin Dhar, has been highly generous in motivating, sharing his personal experiences and helping in launching the book on social networking sites and You Tube.

Much of the credit goes to my grandchild, Aashman Dhar whose innocent emotions and fervour became an impetus to understand the child behaviour and draw inferences on how these manifest into our personality dynamics as we grow in life.

Although children are physically away, but they are true example of "child is the father of man." They were always found inspiring, stimulating and motivating.

I sincerely acknowledge and thank Mr. Arun Kaul, Mrs. Anita Kaul and many dear and near ones, for their continued rallying around and propping up during times of gloom and disappointments.

Last but certainly not the least, Mr. Sahil Gupta, Director, V&S Publishers, Delhi and his team for their belief in the project and constant support and guidance.

– Prof. Bhushan Kachru

"Failure is the mother of success. We all know how mothers are. They nurture us and their constant presence is like an endless inspiration. So live through failures and learn from your crashes, collapses and defeats."

Preface

I offer "The Success of Failure", to all those who feel that they are at a crossroad in their professional life due to personal failures. They may often feel helpless as to what they need to do to march ahead to secure their future. This book is therefore specially written for you and will help you with the insight needed to create and sustain the "Can Do Attitude." Once you learn the truth of how being resilient and hard-wearing works, you will be able to begin building the belief in your self and march ahead with your success campaign.

"The Success of Failure" is a blue print for rebuilding from ground zero on a personal failure and how to turn disappointments and letdowns to success. The ideas and practical suggestions brought forth in this book will be of immense use while undertaking campaigning for success. Remember failure is neither a severe imperfection nor a social syndrome that makes you less valuable. It is a temporary phase of life that may leave you feeling helpless, unhappy, alienated and with greasy soapy feelings. No one, including great kings, leaders, statesmen, warriors, gurus, scientists, administrators, business leaders and politicians have shadowed away from it. In fact, their failures became an aurora of power and a resolution to succeed.

The might of failure is like a night shelter en route to your destination. It is an opportunity to realise a lost dream and to revamp and renovate before you find yourselves at the commencement of a new, dense and robust journey. A failure indeed is a moment of renewal that dispenses you with challenges that may seem futile, but it definitely gives you the fathom to a failing life. Failure doesn't kill you, but makes you mentally stronger to grow a little longer in life. It is a legacy of your past that took place yesterday. So, why sit worrying and moaning? Today is a new dawn and sunrise that has enshrined you with new hope and vigour.

"The Success of Failure" was born out of my experiences gained while undergoing many personal failures and how I was able to convert most of these to success. It was also born out of witnessing confusion, distrust, fear, apathy and droopiness among most people who were not able to accomplish their goals and had met repeated failures in converting their pursuits. Yet, in the midst of all the chaos, failures depicted, there were some who by their power of resilience, perseverance and great determination were able to tame success and bring it home. I also met several individuals and had long conversations to feel their pulse on their failure. Most seemed determined to fight it out, while some lacked motivation and will to stand up and march on their success crusade. They were perhaps lacking in direction as also in guidance and seemed mentally and physically tired. Some were found risk hesitant and did not want to venture out of their comfort zone. I sincerely felt that they needed a push, counselling or coaching.

This book will provide you with a comprehensive insight into a failure's mind-psyche, important guidelines in self-improvement and the ways of combating unconstructive self-beliefs to mitigate the hunger for success. By mastering the simple techniques outlined in the book, you shall not only gain a complete control of your circumstances, but will learn to improve the quality of life. The book contains psychological interventions, practical examples, detailed steps and techniques. It provides author's personal experiences and scores of his success/failure stories to arouse passion and drive within to perform. What is needed though is changing and supplementing the internal mind processes with a new air of thoughts in order to improve your personality, character and attitude through your own efforts and positive mind programming.

"The Success of Failure" attempts to answer most of the doubts, fears and questions you may be confronted with and feel helpless when searching for answers. To incite your interest, numerous illustrations/pictures, quotations and sayings have been included.

The book is based on my more than four decades of practical hands on valuable experience of managing human resources and imparting learning in skill development in some large corporate houses in India. During my professional career, I have interacted, observed and motivated thousands of young minds, including executives, managers, engineers and other professionals from varied backgrounds in their pursuit for success.

Every now and then, one finds several books on how to be successful. The irony however, is that rarely motivational experts have ventured into writing books on how to convert failures to success. This book is therefore my bold attempt and written for those who believe in the beauty of their dreams and want to fulfil the real meaning of life. Wherever 'He' is written, it is applicable to 'She' as well and done for brevity. Behavioural subjects are like a chain, each connected with the other. Some psychological interventions may appear repetitive in the book. This has been done purposely to bring home the point recurringly for its importance and a reminder.

Let each one of you take a pledge of allegiance to self that come what may, you will not give up on your dreams in spite of all obstacles in the past! Rise, shine, and reinvent enthusiasm to get started now.

Let you stand up, dust your mind, rinse and repeat until you succeed! If thousands have been able to accomplish their success campaign after a failure - why not you?

The book comprises of

Part One: - Significance of Failure

Part Two: - Managing Failure

Part Three: - Towards Stitching Success

You are welcome to interact with me through my blog given in my website www.humandynamicsindia.com or interact with me on my mail id: careers@humandynamicsindia.com should you require clarifications or further insights.

– Prof. Bhushan Kachru

Contents

Part-1

Significance of Failure

Don on your Back, Look up, Get up and March Ahead

For most people who haven't experienced any failure, my brief story shall seem a novel ordeal. As a marked event of my life, the memoirs of my failures seem like a face-off with time and an opportunity to move beyond a defeat. With each failure, I have internalised new perspectives on life and have been beneficent of perseverance and the powers of resilience in calibrating the victory of looking beyond sadness and downbeat.

My narrative begins with a reminiscence of my childhood which in many ways was also a phase of my evolvement. I had a humble beginning. I still remember hot summer vacations in 60's in Delhi when me and my siblings would wet it out without having a fan (fan those days was a luxury in middle-class families). I guess I was in 3rd/4th standard. One day, my late father surprised us by bringing a brand new Kassels table fan home on his bicycle. O boy! What a big relief it was as if we had fallen on a treasure hunt. I guess we will not be as happy in buying a new car today as we were on possessing the fan. As I grew up, I turned into a vibrant and extrovert young man. I learnt being resilient and strong when I was young while watching my late father struggle with life in raising the family and yet keeping us happy and contended. I loved and admired my father very much and vowed that I would avoid suffering the kinds of failures that plagued his path. I was incredibly fortunate in my life to have experiences and mentors that showed me how to stand tall and fight it out. For the past several years, I have devoted most part of my life to finding the most effective and practical ways to help young people to rebuild their self-motivation and make over their lives by learning how to live with personal failures and fight it out to get on top of success. However, as time changed, I had many achievements up my sleeves. I was first in many aspects of life in my extended family/ friends/colleagues, etc. Being blessed with the 'gift of gab,' I saw my life sparking. At the young age of 31, I was selected out of several thousand professionals to visit USA on an international fellowship program through a real tough competition in North India.

Surprisingly, life has its own roller coaster. Looking back, I realise that from a timid little boy who listened and observed more and loved to shadow his father, I had turned into a chatterbox with little room for variations of fortune. I remember drawing public attention with my extrovert personality and demeanour, though sometimes my meaningful conversations appeared humorous and amusing, while at other times, these seemed pushy and loud. With a forthright persona, a go-getter attitude, and spunk to achieve, success slowly aggregated in leaps and bounds and I held a senior management position in a large reputed Indian corporate at a young age. In my professional career, I remember being one of the highest paid executives and a notable figure who competed with brilliant minds from the IIT's and the IIM's. I nurtured and trained many amateurs and refined them into adept professionals. I was also blessed with a beautiful family and a caring wife who still holds the anchor of my life. Back then, I seemed to have it all that one desires in the exposition of success. The only thing that I did not have though was the ability to count on hidden failures in my escalation and acceleration to success. Today, however, my fair share of success and failures has revitalised and inspired me to embrace any opportunity or exigency in life.

Reflecting back, my past seems like an era entrapped in the exotic woods with a life that was indeed alluring, yet unsatisfying and sometimes alienating. The many unpredictable events in my life have motivated me to touch the base with who I am, who I became and who I am yet to become. With lessons learnt over time, while some incredible and few others improbable, I have learnt to soak in the lessons of my failures, especially since my life has had a fresh meaning and a new direction. I believe that 'Nature' has been kind to me. It has endowed me with the strength to realise and appreciate the beauty in going downhill and then trying hard to rise towards the summit. In this journey, my conscience and inner spirit to redefine myself has been my eternal companion. In the absence of which, I would have still stuck to my past.

In today's commercially driven society, people measure one's worth on the basis of economic prosperity and material wisdom. However, I have understood the demarcation between making it and losing it and maintaining a calm and balance in between the contrasting strides. I have learnt the lessons of life a hard way, that rich or poor, success or failure, affluence or destitution and sickness or healthy are different phases of life and keep changing. Neither success is permanent nor is failure forever. I have realised that when a person fails, he or she fails the least in public eye, but utmost in one's sentiments and emotions that nurture his/her dreams and desires for a fulfilling and meaningful life.

For most people, who haven't experienced a failure yet, my story shall seem unenthusiastic, gloomy or may even be unexciting. But the truth is that a failure not only teaches a greater lesson than success could ever, but it also makes one patient, improves on staying power, behaviour and above all, a windfall of life experience. One should always remember that sometimes it is the failure that becomes the navigator of a life that we are yet to see. A life lived without a failure is boring and uninteresting. Imagine the kick one gets when failure becomes a pedestal for success. This is in fact the theme of great success stories around the world. Remember, if a tree forgets its root, it will ultimately fall, even though it may appear greener to us on the face of it.

I often imagine had I not faced enduring and difficult times in my life, I would have never imagined of writing this book with a mission to motivate all those whose lives today seem bungled with misadventures. I would once again reiterate that some of my life's greatest lessons are an offshoot of my failures. With my past in the lap of failures, I hear a beckon of a time yet to come, some milestones yet to achieve, and memories of a life coach (my failures) that made me way taller and stronger than I actually was. I learnt my lesson that true vigour does not always lie in standing on the top of a tree, but it actually lies in passionately climbing up the tree. Today when I look back, failure has evolved me and given new and happy directions to my being.

I believe that ***every fighter has one great last fight left in him. I am waiting for that one fight.***

(Author's true story)

CHAPTER 1

Don't Rock Your Boat on a Failure

There's Life in Failure

> *"Striving for success without hard work is like trying to harvest where you haven't planted."*
>
> – *David Bly*

Historically brand success has been the most impressive, astounding and dazzling buzz word around and adored like a shining glass decoration swinging in front of people all the time right from school days. Be it motivational literature, sports and athletics, media, boardroom discussions, etc., every one is reflecting and admiring success stories. Yet surprisingly, I find most people overwhelmingly unhappy, distressed and unable to stand up and stand out in their battle for success. They carry tales of personal failed endeavours and events in their lives. Stressed out and hassled, they are usually chided and mocked because of their perceived sloppiness and slushy performance in accomplishing their success goals. It is said that, **for every success, there are dozens of losers?**

Often in pursuit of accomplishing success goals, you are bound to face repeated failures, stumbling blocks, disappointments and letdowns which are a normal part of your evolving life. These do appear mountainous, encircle you and soon you feel like throwing the towel and the infatuation of blaze within cools off slowly. On one hand you are surrounded by fear and on the other hand, you start searching for reasoning and over and over again your jaded mind says, "O! Gosh what should I do? Why did this happen to me?" Why are you so much annoyed and fearful of failure? Why can't you try and change your mind-set and accept failure gracefully and stop humming and whispering, "Why me?" Isn't failure a normal stopover on your destination to refurbish and repair yourself? **Failure is neither a dead end nor a dark night; it is the beginning of a new dawn and a first light in your renewed dynamism**. Instead of saying, "I have failed!" Say, "I have yet to succeed" or "I am going to succeed." Having taken up a challenge in life why fear failure, why not embrace and learn from it.

On a hindsight, why don't you accept that **failure and hardships are actually good in a way?** With each failure, you internalise new perspectives, become more compassionate, start touching base with your inner spirit, have the joy of finding a 'new you' and build a resilient but humble mind. Moreover, it brings out your inner strengths, weaknesses and makes you realise that the odds will always be there; irrespective of how successful you are. It is rightly said that with every setback, there is a hidden opportunity, so why not try and figure out that opportunity. Sometimes, failure makes you realise your own value and teaches the application of good judgement. Staying with failure is also bravado to be ***"The Man out of Men"*** and you need to dig out your guts to say goodbye to the public perception and getting influenced from the external events and past remembrances. Get out of the usual failure casing as perceived by the common man.

Take cues from the following story of Thomas Edison.

> *"In 1914 Thomas Edison's factory in West Orange, New Jersey, was destroyed by fire and much of Edison's life work went up in smoke and flames. At the height of*

the fire, Edison's son, Charles, searched frantically for his father and found him, calmly watching the fire, his face glowing in the reflection, his white hair blowing in the wind. "My heart ached for him," said Charles. "He was 67 — no longer a young man — and everything was going up in flames."The next morning, Edison looked at the ruins and said, ***"There is great value in disaster. All our mistakes are burned up."*** *Three weeks later, Edison managed to deliver the first phonograph."*

Failure is being tenacious, thirsty for success, desire to survive and be in reckoning no matter what happens. Since there is a mission to accomplish, your mind and body do not get tired out but provide that extra momentum and zeal. I am reminded of Imran Khan, the great cricket legendary from Pakistan who once said that **"I have no fears. Fear of losing my wealth, fear of failure, fear of dying, and that makes me very dangerous for my opponents."** Geet Sethi, the seven times World Billiards Champion once said, **"I am at my best when times are tough, in adversity, not when everything seems fine."** Speaking at the Harvard commencement in 2008, J.K. Rowling, author of the best-selling Harry Potter book series said that "Failure gave me an inner security that I had never attained by passing examinations. Failure taught me things about myself that I could have learnt no other way. I discovered that I had a strong will, and more discipline than I had suspected." Disney, Gandhi, Martin Luther and many others were great failures and they held failures by its horn. They were real dare devils and fear was not in their dictionary, yet every time they failed, they became more resolute and rest is history.

Most people don't like the occasional tasteless existence they live; they simply think there is no choice. Most people don't like the occasional tasteless existence they live; they simply think there is no choice. For example, the recent death of former Bollywood legendary and yesteryear superstar Rajesh Khanna, heart-throb of millions across the country. It is reported that he could not accept his failure from stardom when the blockbuster status changed to poor box office showing of many films he starred during mid seventies and onwards. This is what happens when our mind becomes so obsessed with fantasies and success goes to head. One needs to accept life as a bouquet of happy moments, sad moments and changing moments and each one of us is programmed to pass through these moments. Some one has beautifully put it, **"Life is a one way journey to waste your time mourning on things you can't change. Instead of searching for meanings of why, indulge your time on what and how you'll do next."**

British author Oliver Burkeman, a journalist with *The Guardian* supports my argument in his latest book, 'The Antidote: Happiness for People who can't stand Positive Thinking'. He says that, "Embracing the darker realities of life is as important as imagining a shiny, bright one. Failure is everywhere. It's just that most of the time we would rather avoid confronting that fact." He seems right when he advocates giving a close squeeze and hugging to failure, fear, doubt, glumness and negativity. I feel we need to create a space for failure in our mind. This surely helps to manage failures and makes one prepared in advance to avoid depressions, frustrations and unhappiness at a later date. As is said, "Fore warned are four armed." Some people may feel that failure is far easier to explain compared to success. Possibly yes, if we take the route of destiny. But this need not dither you from working to come back with flying colours. Therefore, understand the meaning of failure and value it. If you make your existence just limited to success-failure, then your goals will always remain confined to your immediate surroundings. Try to unlock your mind, control your emotions and renew faith in yourself. It is then only that you can generate peace within and fight with your disappointments. Admit that you are not the only failure; there are millions like you who fail every day and ultimately succeed. Losing is also winning in that you gave your best, learnt new things, gained useful experience and became chiselled. Appreciate that pain and joy are two cavities of your nose (life) for taking breath. Remember, achievements or failures are only of numerical importance. What matters in the final analysis which should be a stable and happy mind-set that anchors your efforts to accomplish your success campaign.

I know for many it may sound naive to live with the failure. But realise by accepting failure and living with it, you are not only making your mind space rugged to fight ensuing battles, but also giving man's biggest and strongest enemy 'fear' a permanent go by. The day you conquer fear, the battle for success is half won and the challenges will become a cake walk. This is how great athletes turned to historical winners. As motivational coach, Zig Ziglar says, **"Failure is an event, not a person. Yesterday ended last night."**

CHAPTER 2

What is a Failure?

From times immemorial, there probably have been as many failures as the number of attempts made by people towards achieving their short and long-term goals. A series of wrong decisions, choices, lack of hard work, persistency and poor judgements made difficult for many to spring back from. This brings us to the origin of success and the role of failure in achieving success. It certainly is an unimaginable journey wherein scientific developments have been conceived through ordinary ideas like the rubbing of stones to produce fire after a number of failures. Today this incident may be an important part of primary school syllabus, but actually it was the very first attempt of mankind to learn to be successful to save life on the earth. In my view, **failure is like adding water to cement in order to strengthen the foundation of success**. It is not the end, but the end of being disgusted, fearful and demoralised. **Failure is also like the sludge on which the queen of flowers, 'lotus' (success) grows.**

Historically, failure has remained an imaginary ghost, an unfounded fear that haunts every one, unless it is caught by the horns through dedication, purposeful aspiration and above all, the inner drive and consciousness. **Failure is work in progress towards the ultimate goal of accomplishing success.** It is an awakening of your intellect to search alternatives to get over tribulations so that the overflowing sufferings recede and the positive starts taking over the negatives. On a hindsight, wouldn't it be grossly injudicious if you hide yourself from the actual truth that failure bewilders your lives and how much you panic even though you have been programmed for it right from your toddler days. Recall while learning to stand, walk or ride a bicycle how you fell and got up many times on your own because unknowingly you were resilient and persistent and didn't know what quitting was. You innocently hugged failure and adapted till you did what you wanted to. Your mother may have often played the role of a teacher cum motivator, clapped and carried a ray of hope and happiness seeing you pull through the initial and significant stages of life. While on one hand, she kept on saying, "Come on baby, you can walk ok....good. Try again...well." On the other hand, she got lost in her dreams about your future successes and prosperity. While growing up, your granny may have recited stories of legends that experienced success through hard work, honesty and integrity. She, however, may not have introduced you to the tales of failure or legends that could teach you the **'bare and bold'** jerks in life. May be like others, she thought failure was a bad omen, a nightmare and wanted to keep your childhood safe. She didn't realise that by allowing experiencing failure, you would build a tough pedestal to deal with disappointments and letdowns as you move forward in life. Perhaps, she didn't want to disturb your sprouting by making you aware that **life's hard blows are as common as life's achievements.**

There are also times in your lives when you are all geared up and motivated to follow a goal but after working for a brief period, you lose interest to pursue it any further. This is because of 'Amygdala,' a small almond shaped set of nuclei that is part of our mind. It is a limbic system structure that is involved in forming most of our emotions and motivations (panic, rage, happiness, hormonal secretions, arousal, memory, etc.) that are primarily related to our survival. The function of Amygdala is to transmit certain chemicals to the body when needed that generate emotions, such as fear, anxiety, doubt and depression, etc. Amygdala gets sort of signals when we are not comfortable in any characteristic of our life and it acts accordingly. Whenever out of our comfort periphery, we don't like the feelings we experience, we tend to make excuses and hold ourselves back from achieving success.

Failure is not entirely due to the external events affecting your life. On a deeper study of some famous success stories, you would be aghast to know that some of them had to undergo unbearable and horrendous difficulties, yet they made sure that they meet the date with accomplishing their goal. I often feel success and failure in a way are linked to our thoughts, choices and action. Similarly, most people continue being servants of their beliefs and habits which slowly get engrained in their mind-set and consequently become difficult to live without these. Lack of consistency is yet another reason of holding success back. No doubt most perform action in quest for their goals, but actually most of the time they lack **well-defined objective, goal specifics** and focus. They never apply their minds to know why they are on a particular path and where it will lead them to. This is the reason for a large disparity between winners and failures.

Success is neither common nor is it available off the shelf. I have always believed that, **Success is a hard nut to crack and more like searching *nirvana* and *trekking a stony mountain*.** No matter whatever obstacles, setbacks and rejections you face, remember you have a date with your destiny to continue walking and who knows, you may be at a handshake distance to meet your endeavours and fulfil your cherished dream. But how many on a failure are unrelenting, fanatical and frantic to succeed? There are many who daydream success but lack the earnest urge to prove their mettle and courage. Few continue being in the past and are afraid of the unknown, while some feel that a middle of the road approach is a safe bet. Often they don't make it and get wiped out, yet they wag their tails before success. For instance, **a pressure cooker generates steam which is confined and that helps cook food. How many generate enough steam within to move ahead?** Most wait endlessly for things to happen and don't wake up and make things happen. How many possess the killer instincts and hunger for achievement? Stop tolerating whatever holds you back.

Most people become risk-hesitant by doing all sorts of jugglery to escape failure and thus, become detached to experience failure, a necessary part of their development. They don't realise that the gains in life become strong and undithered once they pass through the failure milestone. The early you learn to be risk-prone, the better times lie ahead for you. It is only through risks that you look at new avenues of growing. This is a signpost and indeed imminent and natural teacher that sometimes silently whispers great lessons to help you in your journey. Isn't it absolutely true that, **true dynamism doesn't always lie in standing at the top of a mountain, but actually in climbing to make it to the top?** Your pursuit for accomplishing success is a chain of memorable experiences and events comprising both of success and moments of joy, failure and dejected moments. Failure is simply an action and disappointment, an emotional reaction that happens every now and then and doesn't necessarily define your capability and competence. Failure strikes when you are no more in reckoning and quit. Failure is just a temporary staying down when you trip or stumble on your campaign and you stand defeated should you start believing you can't perform and naturally you start losing on your confidence, motivation and will to achieve. Failure doesn't mean that you're not first-rate; but it does mean that you can improve and become better day by day. Roger von Oech beautifully puts it, **"Remember the two benefits of failure. First, if you do fail, you learn what doesn't work; and second, the failure gives you the opportunity to try a new approach."** For example, a thirsty crow keeps flying from one place to the other in search of water on a hot summer day, but repeatedly fails to fetch water. Does the crow fly back thirsty in the evening and suffer? No, he simply keeps trying by flying in every nook and corner until he succeeds to mitigate his thirst. Every failure in your life is a step towards mitigating your thirst for success.

On a flip side, failure appears to me a miscarriage, a bad dream, a long dark night, running out of luck and an inevitable circumstance. It is as if one has been rapped across the knuckles. Sometimes, I wonder aren't failure like a babe in the woods, surrounded by fear, uncertainties, and desolation? The mind is worn-out and sentiments frozen like ice crystals and you get woven in negative and discouraging thoughts. That's the time when failure takes over you. As some one said that, **"Success is not the result of spontaneous combustion. You have to set yourself on fire."**

Over the years, I presume you would have learnt not to expect clear skies all the time and that failure is an important tool of change. Like thousands, you too would have shared mistakes and failures and were able to convert some to success, while a few turned great opportunities of self-learning and development. In the midst of your path to successes, perhaps you did not comprehend the magnitude of your risks and challenges. Had you not failed, perhaps you would have never realised that life is not only a pillar of success, but a pedestal for failure as well and to acknowledge the soul of your last fight-**'Perform or Perish'**. When you look back at your career or otherwise, you may have a feeling of immense satisfaction at what you have managed to achieve. However, over the years, the experiences of failure and success has helped you to reshape your beliefs and actions in ways that seem to have toughened you and brought humility. "I for one have realised that the belief in self and will to perform enabled me to take the risks that led to some of my proudest accomplishments. I have known that the challenge to accomplish dreams lie in approaching each new day with a transformed thought activated with determination, patience, persistence and self-motivation. I have learnt more from failures than success. Many times, what appeared awful in the beginning actually turned out to be a blessing later? I always keep reminding myself that a **'Derby race horse doesn't get entangled in bushes but keeps galloping ahead no matter what happens?'**. Remember, yesteryear blockbuster 'Rocky' and how Sylvester Stallone working as a small time boxer is ridiculed, mocked, and called a bum in the film. Losing few games, Rocky fights his way to heavyweight champion of the 'World Apollo Creed'. This was a moment of his reckoning to fight for success.

Let us look at failure from a slightly different perspective. The law of attraction states that whatever you hold your attention on, you will attract. But ask a failure, he feels that this is all humbug, a philosophy and a theory. It is unbelievable for him to realise that the failure may be a blessing in disguise and who knows it may turn upheaval into triumph, a perspective difficult to predict when in commotion. But that was yesterday! As soon as a new crack of dawn sets in, it usually comes up with a new hope and vigour to start a new chapter. It is as if **'April showers brought forth May flowers'**. A new Avatar is born that glues the hurdles. With fire in the belly and strength in the nerves, you are here to fight it out with life and snatch success. It's like being with a changed mind-set and not putting the 'cart before the horse'. A new passion infuses and signals you to **'Get, Set, and Go'** to fight it out. It's time to **'Waka Waka'** (Cameroonian dialect, meaning Do it!). You eagerly wait for action to ignite with some extremely hard punches to push. Few years back, I was interviewing an export professional for a senior opening for an auto-component manufacturing company. While interviewing, I was stunned to hear him out:-

> *"After graduating in engineering and clearing GRE with high percentile, I was offered admission in MS in engineering in an Ivy League university in the US. My parents had a dream to send me to US right through my childhood. My father was working as a teacher and had saved money right through to see me a foreign qualified engineer. My parents cried when they came to see me off at the Chennai airport. All through the flight, I was dreaming life at the Ivy League University. There seemed happiness and success all around. Once the flight taxied in at the JFK airport in New York, I went to the immigration counter and suddenly, the evil of failure and ill luck struck me like a lightning and cloudburst. On the way, some one*

had stolen my passport and visa papers. I was detained at the airport for several hours before instructed to take back the same flight I had come. I am still not able to figure out how success changed hands so blatantly."

Success and failure are like brothers and have the same parentage, and their story starts the day you were born when your parents might have compared you with the other newborns in the hospital nursery. Right from childhood, parents put you under pressure to perform more out of comparisons and competition and less out of nurturing success as a way of life. But imagine, if there was no failure, success would be more of an optical illusion. The famous song sung by great Indian singer Manna Dey in 70's **"Zindagi, kaisi yeh paheli hai, kabhi yeh hasaye, kabhi yeh rulaye"** (Life is a puzzle, just as it gives you reason to smile, it also makes you weep sometimes), a beautiful lyric that actually sums up the saga of success - failure.

To be honest, success and failure happens every day in your lives. Unfortunately, your minds are so occupied and evolved that you neither notice nor realise several slips or correct things you undertake as part of your daily routine. It is an irony that you either repeat mistakes or commit new ones every hour, every day, yet you appear to be least concerned because you may feel, **'It hardly matters.'** How prized are the words of wisdom of some great soul who once summed up the success-failure tale, **"The elevator to success is out of order; we will have to use the stairs, one step at a time."** The demarcation between success and failure is no doubt thin and fragile. Erasing this demarcation is solely dependent on how soon you charge and activate yourself, become desperate, strategise your moves, discipline your mind and be optimistic of achieving your success campaign. Like the game of cricket, success-failure is full of uncertainties. There are times when success is an underdog and emerges from nowhere as was the case with the Pakistan cricket team at the 1992 Cricket World Cup in Australia.

I am reminded of Tom Peter's best-selling book, 'In Search of Excellence' wherein he states that the three key components of success are: **"Test Fast, Fail Fast, and Adjust Fast."** Tom's insight on success-failure relationship and advocating need to keep trying new avenues to manage failure without fear and learn from each fault to ultimately hit the bull's eye is of immense relevance. Successful are always found making tough resolutions that are out of reach of the common people. They always focus on finding solution to the obstacle, while handfuls of failures see every obstacle as problem and excuse not to perform. Success at the cost of personal upheavals of any kind whatsoever ultimately leads to worst failure in life. One looks to celebrities as role models and when cans of worms start trickling, people feel bemused, appalled and resentful. A beautiful quote by Barkha Dhar, a young published writer in the US sums it in a lucid way, **"People may be mighty riches externally yet may be mighty rags within."** The moral is that don't measure someone's success by his/her celebrity status, exterior postures and a life lead out of fairy tales. Evaluate in totality, the inside out of their success.

CHAPTER 3

The Positive Power of Failure

Since the dawn of civilization, human minds have been moulded in such a way that one is expected to win at all costs and bring laurels as much to himself as to his family/organization. Ironically, humans have been programmed since childhood to lay high premium on success and look down upon failure as a defeated, non-performer and unlucky (this mind-set needs changing). You are made to believe that winning means a round of applause, bursting of crackers and media hype. The winners are garlanded, become page one stories and we often say, 'aha what pleasant news', while losers are told, "Well try your luck next time." They get boots or rotten tomatoes and feel like carrying hara-kiri and sooner are 'out of sight out of mind'. The ones who are anxious, willed, devoted and unwavering after overcoming distress see losing as an opportunity of rebuilding from ground zero to be on road to success. A visit to scriptures and mythological tales reminds us that even the messengers of God had to experience failure at the hands of demons before truth could conquer the evil.

As said earlier, success and failure are undoubtedly relative terms. For example, those students who manage excellent grades in their examinations glitter with success, but not getting admission in their preferred institution for higher learning is experiencing failure in a way. Similarly, an annual remuneration of Rupees Three lakhs($ 6000) may be success for an individual, but for another, it may be a failure because he is expecting an annual remuneration of

Rupees Five lakhs($10,000). Similarly some of you can be on a high pedestal in your respective careers, but may consider your self-failure because you lost the race for the coveted position in the organisation or a team declared runners up in a tournament, etc. Failure small or big, no doubt seems an irritant beyond your control on many occasions, yet as time passes, you learn to live with these impediments in your stride and hope for sunny days ahead.

On a hindsight, have you ever realised that the percentage of failures is enormously high in almost all professions including sports, athletics, management, education, media, cinema, reality shows and business, etc? Take for example, the corporate world, against the vacancy of a manager advertised; hundreds of applications from aspiring candidates are received. After a gruelling selection process, only few are shortlisted for the final interview and only one among them is finally selected and offered the job. In a way, rest are failures at least for that particular job opening. According to a study reported by *The Guardian* (28 December, 2009), 78% respondents in a survey failed to live up to their new year resolutions because of lack of commitment to their goal, wishful thinking and lack of knowledge and will to understand how self-improvements really works out. For example, in the US, it is said that entrepreneurs fail three to five times before they actually start a business that succeeds. *According to the U.S. Small Business Administration, over 50%* of *small businesses fail in the first year and 95% fail within the first five years*. Similarly, out of the four lakh fifty-six thousand(0.45 million) candidates who appeared in the IIT-JEE examination conducted in 2010 in India, only thirteen thousand one hundred four candidates were declared qualified to seek admission in various IIT'S across India, i.e., a pass percentage of 2.87. These brief facts bring home the reality that in attaining goals, most people fail and there are thousands of failure stories which may not be reported. Perhaps, people don't like to share experiences that don't depict them in good strides and also the influence of external events. For instance, authors Hyatt and Gottlieb interviewed about 200 professionals in many fields for their book, 'When Smart People Fail' and found most had experienced professional failures due to poor interpersonal skills, wrong fit, lack of commitment, self-destructive behaviour, poor management skills, and bad luck. For example, Henry Ford, R. H. Macy, Oprah and Walt Disney are mentioned for having several unsuccessful business ventures before they figured out how to lead successful companies. The Oscar Award winner, Bert Salzman once said, "I actually consider my failure to become a feature film director as the beginning of what I consider a saner and more successful life. After winning the Oscar, I had visions of going right to the top, and when I didn't get there immediately; I began to reconsider my life."

Failures can be small or big. Small failures are part of your daily nitty-gritty and are easily absorbed without affecting your image and sooner forgotten. However, some failures get stuck to your mind and remain for long time trapped. At times, failure becomes most damaging when in spite of going all out on your success campaign with full self-confidence and determination, yet you don't make it. The sufferings that accompany failure can be acute and soon you start with a negative thought 'what happens if I can't.' I am reminded of a popular British film, 'Chariots of Fire' released in 1981, depicting the fact-based story of two athletes who compete in the 1924 Olympics. Runner Abrahams who had prepared industriously runs to overcome prejudice but loses. On not making a mark, he turns to his girlfriend and in a stunned and sad murmur confesses that, "I just don't think I can run any faster." Sense of failure in such or similar situations is most painful and carries persistently for long time and can be overcome sooner if you are able to achieve a big success. But the everlasting reality is that ... **Yesterday you were a failure, today you are successful, tomorrow you may fail again... and this will keep on going.** This reminds me of following incident reported by Shekhar Kapur, the renowned film director.

During the release of Bollywood film, 'Ishq Ishq Ishq' in 1974, one evening Dev Anand was excited taking calls from the press and the distributors congratulating him on the excellent opening his film had made. But over the next two hours, the tone changed, face looked sad, jubilation was over and voice turned softer and lifeless. The calls which subsequently followed spoke of failure of the film at the box office and slowly the telephone turned silent and the room was filled with loneliness of failure. Dev Anand had put almost all his money into the venture and had lost all of it. Then the calls stopped. No one called and the loneliness of failure hung in the room. But within ten minutes, he controlled himself, stabilised his mind, reinvented his killer instinct of fighting back and started brain storming for his next venture. His eyes were vibrant and face excited. He was unable to sit down in his excitement. The ghost of failure and gloom had immediately been changed to a new hope, aspirations and will to fight. *(Excerpts:http://shekharkapur.com/blog/2011)*

Failure always comes up with a message, but majority don't explore the message and instead become fearful of how others will react to their failure. Some find it hard to accept, for them it is a liability, disappointment and disillusionment. They are always found justifying their failed attempts and passing over the blame. Accepting failure is an endowment and a boon to dispassionately look at your weaknesses and endurance levels and how your approach is going to be different next time. Sometimes, your inner voice and natural feelings keep giving pointers that **'you can bounce back, keep at it and move on.'** How you respond to the negative feedback is of utmost importance and can decide your future course of action.

Success, whether small or big no doubt remains the most important mission of every one's life; it is also elemental to the scientific developments around the world. For example, the landing of man on the moon and return is a sheer outcome of success after undergoing repeated failures! Success undoubtedly is like an established trade name that has not only goodwill, but also a brand equity that takes one to the top in one's career. While this understanding of success is common and also important for the welfare of humanity, it also sometimes makes one tardy and even complacent in life. Wouldn't you wish that you had a cushy job and a bank account that made life easier and at par with the successful people around? But would that successful part of you has ever realised the fundamentals to success and the reason to failure. More importantly, it would have never made you think to keep moving and hunting that one chance to bounce back in life and transform past failures and mistakes into a catalyst for success. You may be at times wondering why people run away from failure, be a headless chicken and put away the resolve to confront failure. It is because of their mind programming right from childhood. (For details, see chapter 12.)

Another important perspective of failing may be understood when you often speculate how the next door guy is able to confront failure and make it a podium for accomplishing success, but "I am not?" Wait a minute and ask youself-**"How many times have I missed my good night sleep and kept working on my goal? How many times have I missed a date with my beloved and instead continued working on my campaign? How many times have I missed my lunch and dinner and kept dispassionately working? How many times have I missed to watch a blockbuster movie with my family and instead be on my work station to convert my failure to success? How many times have I continued working in extreme hot and sultry weather covered with sweat from top to bottom and yet kept my focus and urge to surge?"** The next door guy often does this. It possibly is his way of life and habit of taking failure head on seriously. Irving Stone, a famous novelist was once asked what runs through the lives of all great exceptional people. He said, "They are beaten over the head, knocked down, vilified and for years, they get nowhere. But every time they're knocked down, they stand up. You cannot destroy these people. And at the end of their lives, they've accomplished some modest part of what they set out to do." No doubt, it's hard getting up after a couple of knock-downs but achieving success is like a difficult rope climb up in the mountains. How quickly and consistently you get back on ycur toes and not quit decides your future course of climbing. Late Vince Lombardi, a famous football coach in the US once said that, **"It's not whether you get knocked down; it's whether you get back up. Just never quit!"** Jamie Dimon, chief of JP Morgan once said, "Every one has their ups and downs. Tell me one person you admire, not just in business, but in life, and you will find they had their share. Nelson Mandela walked out of prison after twenty seven years, magnanimous to his captors. You have to get up, brush yourself and move on."

From my personal experience, I feel a sizable percentage of people grow with a mind-set consisting of feelings and beliefs that often make them confused and directionless throughout life. Successful people don't use a magic wand or some sort of a success formula or possess a Midas touch. They put heart and soul in accomplishing their goal. **They are always eager to catch the fish in the first go because they realise that time is their biggest resource**. Even if they fail in their attempt, yet they don't lose heart and become frustrated and coax their luck. They go back to the starting line, evaluate their pitfalls, keep trying repeatedly and are with their goal each moment of their life no matter even if it takes months or years to reach finally their destination. That is how they are in charge of themselves and ultimately cross the finishing line and stand out tall and deliver. These daredevils have a will to perform and are not comfortable in being back benchers, a habit some of you might have developed right from your schooldays. Sumner M. Redstone, former Chairman of Viacom, one of the world's largest entertainment and media organizations once said how his early failures helped him to get where he is today, **"Big success is not built on success. It's built on adversity, failure and frustration, sometimes catastrophe and the way we deal with it and turn it around."** Ask youself how you are going to rebuild your self from ground zero and make failure your memorable pedestal for success.

Failing and making mistakes is a process of evolving, but not learning from it is somewhat being close to dementia. Wilma Rudolf's dazzling quote should act as a great inspiration to all those who want to move beyond failure that, **"Winning is great, sure, but if you are really going to do**

something in life, the secret is learning how to lose. Nobody goes undefeated all the time. If you can pick up after a crushing defeat, and go on to win again, you are going to be a champion someday." Let me share the following interesting story on overcoming adversities and hardships in life:-

Once a depressed young woman went to her mother with trails of struggles she was undergoing and felt like giving up. The mother went to the kitchen and filled three pots with water and placed these on fire and the pots came to boil. In the first, she placed carrots, in the second, she placed eggs and in the last, she placed ground coffee beans and allowed these to boil. Little later on, she turned off the burners and fished these out and placed these in separate bowls. She asked the daughter, "Tell me, what you see?" "Carrots, eggs and coffee," she replied. The mother asked her to feel the carrots which had turned soft. Next, she asked her to take an egg and break it. After peeling off the shell, she observed the hard-boiled egg. Finally, the mother asked the daughter to sip the coffee. The daughter tasted its rich aroma. The daughter then asked, "What does it mean?" The mother said that, "each of these objects had faced the same adversity ... boiling water and each reacted differently. The carrot went in strong, hard and unrelenting. However, after being subjected to the boiling water, it softened and became weak. The egg had been fragile. Its thin outer shell had protected its liquid interior, but after sitting through the boiling water, its inside became hardened. The ground coffee beans were unique, however. After these were in the boiling water, they had changed…the water. "Which are you?" she asked her daughter.

Moral

Whenever you undergo failures, adversities or struggles in life, how do you respond decides the fate of the adversity and whether you allow these to affect your moving ahead in life. Therefore, are you a carrot, an egg or a coffee bean?"

Great leaders shaped the destiny of their nations and took success-failure as part of their life mission. They firmly believed that, "**Anyone can give up; it's the easiest thing in the world to do. But to hold it together when everyone else would understand if you fell apart, that's true strength."** The more they visualised success, the more it became obvious that the only option available was to attack. Many a time, they were down under but their resolve to succeed and a date with history made them to come back and fight. There are thousands of stories of individual failures who ultimately made their failure as a pedestal, for dazzling success. For example, Kishore Biyani founder of Future Group(India) had a number of failures to begin with. His yarn factory had gone out of action in the early 1990's. This was followed by his branded apparel business and his struggles initially with Pantaloon departmental store. In 2000, his turn around came when he read, *'Made in America'*, Wal-Mart founder Sam Walton's autobiography. Since then, there has been no looking back. With guts and business instincts, he created *Future Group, a $1 billion company that includes Pantaloon Retail, a department store group; Big Bazaar, the company's name for hypermarkets; Food Bazaar supermarkets, and Central Mall. Known for his insights into the Indian consumer behaviour, he is called "the Sam Walton of India,* (Excerpts: businessworld.in & /knowledge.wharton.upenn.edu). Take the case of Li Ka-Shing, born in poverty in China and moved to Hong Kong. He lost his father at a young age and was forced to leave school and find job in a plastics trading company where he laboured 16 hours a day. By 1950 he was able to start his own company which he developed into a leading real estate investment company in Hong Kong. Li was named "Asia's Most Powerful Man" by Asia week in 2001. His companies make up 15% of the market cap of the HK Stock Exchange. Take for instance the rise and fall of Donald Trump who made a fortune in real estate in the 1980s and early 1990s in the US through resilience and smart moves by keeping a tap at what was happening in the market place. However, due to slump in the real estate business in the late 1990s, Donald Trump's personal fortune was gone and he was US$900 million in debt. The banks moved in to make him bankrupt. However, as luck would have it, the late 1990s saw the revival in his financial situation and fame. In 2001, he completed the Trump World Tower, a 72-storey residential tower across from the U N Headquarters. In the recent past, Steve Jobs, the great innovator's name as a failure and then being at the top of success is really an eyeopener. He was driven out of the same company, Apple which he set up in the mid-80s and struck with cancer when he was at the pinnacle of his success. Behind Steve's success flag, there were innumerable failures of product designs, commercial and functional failures of products. General George Patton once during world war said that, **"I don't measure a man's success by how high he climbs but how high he bounces when he hits the bottom."**

Sir Winston Churchill was defeated fighting for every public office in UK until he became the prime minister at the age 62. The Oxford University once asked him to address its commencement programme. As he approached the podium, the crowd rose in appreciative applause. He gazed at his waiting audience and shouted, **"Never give up!"** Several seconds passed before he rose to his toes and repeated: **"Never give up!"** and left the platform keeping the audience puzzled. Not many people know that in 1952, Sir Edmund Hillary first attempted to climb the Mount Everest, but failed. A few weeks later, a group in England asked him to address its members. Hillary walked on stage to a thunderous applause. The audience was recognising an attempt at greatness, but Edmund Hillary saw himself as a failure. He moved away from the microphone and walked to the edge of the platform, and made a fist pointing at a picture of the mountain. He said in a loud voice, **"Mount Everest, you beat me the first time, but I'll beat you the next time because you've grown all you are going to grow... but I'm still growing!"** Sir Edmund Hillary finally became an epitome of success of failure by becoming the first man to climb the Mount Everest on May 29, 1953. (Source: Edmund Hillary -High Adventure). Thomas Watson, founder of IBM, once said that, **"You can be discouraged by failure or you can learn from it. Go make mistakes.**

Because that's where you will find success." The all time great basketballer Michael Jordan missed more than 9000 shots in his illustrious career and lost almost 300 games. **"I've failed over and over again in my life. And that is why I succeed."** A fascinating experience of failure is that of J.K. Rowling, author of the best-selling *Harry Potter* book series. Delivering her commencement address at the Harvard Alumni Association in 2008, she said that, "What I feared most for my self at your age was not poverty, but failure. However, the fact that you are graduating from Harvard suggests that you are not very well-acquainted with failure. You might never fail on the scale I did, but some failure in life is inevitable. It is impossible to live without failing at something, unless you live so cautiously that you might as well not have lived at all – in which case, you fail by default."

Talking about the power of resilience, being unbending and undeterred on a failure, I am reminded of a childhood story of a group of frogs moving through a jungle. Two frogs from the group fell in a deep pit and other frogs surrounded the pit to see what was happening and kept on shouting that the two were as good as dead. The two frogs ignored the comments and tried to jump out of the pit with all their might. Finally, one of the frogs took heed to the advice and gave up. He fell down and died. The second frog continued to jump as hard as he could in spite of the shouts to stop jumping. He continued with his resilience and started jumping even harder and finally succeeded and got out. On coming out of the pit, the other frogs said, "Did you not hear us?" The second frog said, "I was deaf. I thought you were encouraging me all the time." This is the outcome of a persistent and unyielding mind.

There are thousands of stories of moving from despair to success. However, I am somewhat fascinated from the following inspiring true stories (in brief) which are hair rising and finest examples of daring endurance, risk taking, zeal, optimism and 'never give up attitude'. Several other stories on success of failure in brief are given in Chapter 26.

- *Naga Naresh Karutura spent his childhood in poverty in Teeparru, a small village in Andhra Pradesh. Though his parents were illiterate, yet they instilled in him the importance of education. "I remember finishing my schoolwork fast in class and sleeping on the teacher's lap!" On January 11, 1993, his mother took him to a nearby village for a family function. On the way, he fiddled with the lorry's door latch and it opened wide throwing him out and he met with an accident. He underwent surgery and subsequently, due to neglect of wounds, gangrene developed. In no time, both his legs were amputated up to the hips. "I remember waking up and asking my mother, where are my legs? I was in the hospital for three months. I don't think my life changed dramatically after I lost both my legs. I was enjoying all the attention rather than pitying myself." In school, he was inspired by two people; his Mathematics teacher who encouraged him to participate in various local talent tests and a brilliant senior student who had joined a tutorial institute to prepare for IIT-JEE. It became Naga Naresh's dream too. Moving to a residential school was a big change for him. It was the first time that he was on his on. As luck would have it, Naga Naresh met a boy who was in the top 10 in IIT-JEE exams and he inspired him to prepare for getting into IIT. Though his overall rank in the IIT-JEE was not high, yet he was 4th in the physically handicapped category and joined IIT, Madras (Chennai). He was sent to Boston for internship by the institute. He passed out of IIT Madras (Chennai) and joined Google in Bangalore (Bengaluru).*

- *The story of Karthika Annamalai from Tamil Nadu, India is a fine example of 'never give in attitude'. Born to an extreme poor quarry worker, Karthika grew in a mud hut and would walk about covering her face from mud roads with her skirt lifted shamelessly over her head. As a child she would sit nearby and keep gazing at her mother who worked at a quarry shattering stones. She joined Shanti Bhavan School and would spend all her time in visualising which resulted in her receiving various awards for her passion for art. While in school, she was taught to face challenges and believe in self which has over the years got ingrained in her psyche. How Karthika remarkably over came severe odds and joined an elite group that of CLAT by cracking the Indian Common Law Admission Test, 2011 is both fascinating and inspiring. As she reflects on the past 14 years of her life, she realises these are tied to one of her two lives – that of a village girl who grew up in a world of sadness, desperation and devoid of hope and the other, of an educated and confident woman, who was given an amasing opportunity to aspire.(Ref: www. shantibhavanonline.org/children/karthika.html)*

- *In 1982 Steven Callahan, an experienced sailor was crossing the Atlantic in his sailboat. He was in a race from Penzance to the Canary Islands. One night, while lying in his bunk, he heard a huge cracking sound and water started rushing in. He at first ran up to the deck to see what had happened. He realised that Solo was sinking very fast. He grabbed everything that he could scavenge in the short amount of time. He had just three-pounds of food and eight pints of fresh water but he did have many supplies to help him stay alive including a spear and two water distillers. The first couple days were a struggle to figure out and decide how to survive out at sea. The very first boat that he had spotted he shot off eight flares hoping to get the boats attention but the boat went right by. Over the next couple of months six other boats passed him. On the forty-third day the bottom of his raft flooded due to a huge hole. Even though he was extremely tired and exhausted for thirty-three days when three fishermen found him, He had lived seventy-six days out at sea in his raft that he had called Rubber Ducky. (Ref: Steven Callahan. Adrift: Seventy-six Days Lost at Sea. New York: Ballantine Books, 1996).*

Callahan wrote in his book, 'Adrift' that, "Compared to what others have been through, I'm fortunate. **I tell myself these things over and over, building up fortitude. You should never give up even if you are down physically and mentally and that you should go to your grave trying to survive. The strong shall survive and the weak shall die."** I am reminded of conversation by Paul Bettany in Hollywood movie "Legion" which should act a great source of inspiration to all those who stand in the middle of a crossroad, not knowing what to do on a failure, **"in the midst of all this darkness, I see some people who will not be bowed. I see some people who will not give up, even when they know all hope is lost. Some people, who realise being lost is so close to being found."**

You may often feel that your struggles are far ahead of others and feel agitated and paranoiac? If this is the mind-set, how will you really accomplish what you have been cherishing all these years? Isn't failure a minor faltering block, a correction to take the right direction on way to success? Why be afraid of getting anything wrong. **There is no wrong or right, it is all in the mind. After all, right follows wrong and dawn follows night... Failure happens in every one's life. But how you deal with it seems a million dollar question.** Before deciding to call it a day and hang your dreams, just remember that time doesn't wait for any one and that opportunity lost once is lost forever. Wouldn't you therefore like to hit the iron when it is hot? Wouldn't it be necessary and important to move beyond failure? **Surely if you believe in your self, oceans become rivulets and mountains turn hillocks. Just think?**

Powerful Outcome of Failure

- Failure is a *mantra* of desperation, a rosary bead that activates devotion and commitment to act and accomplish your mission.
- It is launching of fire that fuels your inner urge to perform. It is a path finder and a spiritual guru that advises how to tread the path for success. It turns failure to 'Hall of fame' and teaches *mantras of tolerance, resolution and calmness.*
- It is not an undertaker but a message of God to look for answers within and explore new routes to achieve the goal. This *gives strength to withstand crisis, innumerable pressures and frustrations which are the baggage of failure.*

My idea finds support from well-known Greek author Plutarch who opines that, **"What we achieve inwardly will change outer reality."**

- Failure is a hope that **'every cloud has a silver lining.'** It brings you close to realise the feelings of thousands who fail every now and then and succeed.
- Challenges you to think and activates new ideas and paths to reach your ultimate destination. For example, a basketball player right from the beginning develops a mental image of putting the ball in the basket. Every time, he is close to the basket, he becomes desperate to put the ball in. This desperation is an outcome of his visualisation right from childhood and often leads to success.
- Failure is not cast in stone, it is written on snow and the moment there is sunshine in your endeavours, it gets erased. It is also written on sand and one big wave of your desperation erases it.
- A response to your actions, reactions and the moment you change your perspectives, swimming from a pond to a river is just a matter of time.
- At times steps to steer your failure may look small and shaky. But remember, it is only '**small waves that build the mammoth current'** that is unbeatable.
- All success stories, in fact are an outcome of stories of great failures.
- If by chance, one has not tasted failure, believe me, he has been unfortunate not to live a life of challenges against high tides and developing a strong mind-set. As Edison said a century ago, **"I am not discouraged, because every wrong attempt discarded is another step forward."**
- Failure is a force that redirects you to the starting line. Don't ever retire but get on to the place of action, take risks, fall, get up and continue playing, fight harder to come back and cross the finishing line.

- Failure is an opportunity to stir up self through experiences of trial, let down and sufferings to get inspired. After all, steel becomes finer only after put through the hottest furnace.
- Failure and success move parallel and are the two sides of a coin, just like tossing a coin in a cricket or soccer game- 'heads we win and tails you lose.' At times, I perceive the success-failure relationship similar to the game of chess, where one wrong move can end up losing scores. I have been forced to believe that success-failure is more close to playing a game of snakes and ladders in its essence and outcome. It is like night and day, dusk and dawn or fall and spring.
- There is no guarantee against failure as there is no guarantee against success. Just like success can hit a failure anytime or any point in life, similarly, failure can hit a successful person, a high flier any time in life. After all, **'Every stick has two ends'**.

If you are happy to harvest a good crop of success, why cry on a cropless season of failure? Isn't harvesting a good crop or a season of draught reality of life? Don't you need to learn to live both happiness on success and pain on a failure uniformly because each is dependent on the other? Thousands have failed; they lived with it, but never thought that they were failures. 'They rebuilt from ground zero to move beyond failures' like the true warriors and ultimately, reached their destination. They were real "Dabangs"(dare devils). Can you try to be like them?

CHAPTER 4

Failure opens up Many Routes to Success

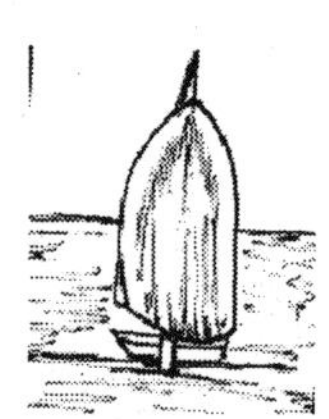

As you grow in life and become independent, you start gradually moving from the passenger seat(comfort zone) to the driver's seat(action zone) of your mind chariot? You start eagerly looking forward to be the driver of your own self, thoughts, desires and destiny. Your life choices slowly start getting activated and by the law of nature, some of these don't give the desired outcome and you become agitated to the hilt not knowing what to do next and your mind seems distracted, paranoid and suddenly life appears paralytic. It is possible that the alternative you decided was not necessarily the right option. But why abandon your chase? Isn't letdown a pointed test on your perseverance, commitment and willpower to do what it takes and your ability to move over, around, bypass and turn obstacles into advantages? Often your desire to get to your destination may not be strong enough backed by an iron will. Naturally you allow obstacles to sway you from your path and make an erroneous assumption that there wasn't another coarse open to you. Someone has rightly said that, **"The road to success may be rocky, but without the rocks, you're on a different road.**

The path of struggles and your efforts to overcome these at time may appear like an unending sail by a boat through twists, turns and often cruising against the howling winds. These twists and U-turns often bring challenges to navigate. Having a U-turn in life may not always mean failure; it essentially is a 'wake up call.' U-turns are significant, frequently life-altering and a road map of your transformation by undergoing change of observation, habits and self-renewal. Most of the time, letdowns and disappointments are opportunities in disguise to reevaluate your route that allows you to make the changes in your success campaign to reach your goal. The path of your success campaign is not always a straight line; it is full of speed breakers/path holes/hindrances and off course smooth rides as well. No one really knows when a U-turn will come. You have an option to become deserter and turn back home or keep walking, the choice is yours.

History is witness to the fact that **'Failure is the mother of Success'** and that the real macho in you comes out only in hardships. That is why it is said that, **God throws you into deep waters, not to drown you, but to test you in bottomless situations**. Life at each stage is like a game, some win, some lose and those who lose need to rearm and fight back to win. But as you grow, some start looking for short-cuts to accomplishments without realising that there are more chances of U-turns subsequently. In my view, using failure as a stepping stone to success is like that U-turn mostly from a dead end that inspires you to build a bridge or dig out a tunnel to reach to the other side. As someone has rightly said, **"to bend in the road is not the end of the road unless you fail to make the turn."** There are innumerable examples of people who start as an average in their academic pursuits or profession, but a time comes in their lives, when whatever they touch turns to unbelievable success because of change of direction in following their passion. Success is not just paddling the accelerator; it is a dedication and lifetime commitment of fuelling your infatuation and excitement to win the race. As Ron Finklestein once said, "Your success and my success are totally dependent on how well we communicate, influence, motivate, lead, counsel, mentor, sell and persuade those we deal with on a daily basis."

Failure will always exist in every nook and corner, but can you tolerate being ripe and yet rotting? If there are snags that are preventing you to move ahead, self-assess or take advice to objectively look for what's holding you back. It may sound naïve in today's fast forward life, where every one around wants to step on your toes and be in a hurry to reach their goals. But I still firmly believe that you need to walk the journey like the tortoise and be focussed and firm to get to the finishing line, no matter whatever comes in your way.

Don't take Failure as a Curse

Most people are crestfallen after the first failed attempt; some try again once or twice, then lose hope and become desperate. The difference between the ones, who continue trying until they succeed and those who decide to retreat is their perception of failure and feeling that they are at the dead end of the road. Thousands undertake their success campaign with an earnest hope that they will make it. But most are thrown back to their point of start battered. Some of them feel that their attempts to move forward in their career at times negatively dictate that they shouldn't have dared to dream outside of their periphery. They feel that **success has many fathers, but failure none.** Repeated failures are like a caution signal since you become branded until you improve, change and continue fighting the 'battle of the budge.' There are innumerable examples of repeated personal failures on account of health, business, examinations, relationships and meeting personal objectives, etc. Often lack of enthusiasm, low gusto, aggravation of highest order, discouragement, etc. are the feelings people go through. It creates a major self-doubt of whether they would at all be able to meet their objectives. It is like **knotted with failure, but hunting for success**. Such feeling seems natural, but not justified. If you are a fighter and filled with resolution, possess tenacity and patience, you will surely stand up and get over the feelings of distress and hatred. Some readers may feel that it is hypocrisy. But remember, isn't it better than quitting and grousing? In a society that places such high premium on success, there is no room for feelings such as cursing, weeping and moaning.

I once read the story of Thomas Edison and found out that he failed more than 10000 times when trying to create a light bulb. When asked about it, Edison said, "I have not failed 10000 times. I have successfully discovered 10000 ways to NOT make a light bulb." Each failure in life *is a value addition and adds on in life. For example,* the IAS topper in 2011, Ms. S. Divyadharshini had her second attempt at the prestigious examination as she failed in the first attempt but continued with her dream. Vidit, CAT topper of 2011 was able to make it in his third attempt to qualify for IIMs. Take a look at K. Jayaganesh's(IAS) story of repeated failures.

> *K. Jayaganesh was brought up in a poor family in a village in Vellore district. After his 10th standard, he joined a polytechnic college and passed out with 91 per cent marks and subsequently, joined government engineering college to study graduation in mechanical engineering. After completing his engineering in 2000, he went to Bangalore (Bengaluru) and got a job on a meager salary of Rupees 2,500(US$60) per month. "I was not having enough money to buy even proper food." He resigned and went home to prepare for the IAS examination. In his first two attempts, he could not even clear the preliminary examination. He tried to get a job as an engineer but failed. He then took up a part time job as a billing clerk at a cinema hall and also worked as the server during the interval. In the last attempt, finally when the results came, he secured the 156th rank out of more than 700 selected candidates and got into IAS. Jayaganesh's story is that of an unyielding mind.* (Excerpts: upscmantra.com)

Late Jim Rohn - the great motivational guru – developed what he called the 'Ants Philosophy'. He identified four key lessons based on ant's behaviour- Ants never quit, ants think winter all summer, ants think summer all winter and ants do all they possibly can. Can you learn from the ant's stride and become wiser to act on your next move and not rest till you convert your repeated failures to a memorable success?

Part-2

Managing Failures

Don't get Haunted by the Fear of Failure

The negative experiences generated due to a failure often haunt most people with fear, panic and apprehensions. Fear of failure makes the biggest, the brightest and the commoners beat about it every now and then. Sometimes, I feel fear of failure is worse than the failure itself. The fear puts your mind space to so many imaginary scenarios and unfounded worries that often frighten and render you standstill. At times, fear also occurs due to continuous negative internal dialogues, your childhood experiences, poor understanding of success mechanism, inadequate handling of emotions and beliefs, panic of rejection, being emotionally sensitive, etc. These get registered gradually in your subconscious mind and subsequently form a major part of your negative feelings and beliefs that become obstacles in life. Each one is different in the things and situations one fears; find out what kinds of fears bothers you? For example, the decision to make a major career change or appearing in an examination / job interview can trigger all kinds of anxiety. "What if I fail?" This is exactly what happened with Natalia Pogonina, Russian chess woman Grand Master during the Women's European Chess Championship-2011 in Tbilisi. She did succeed but committed few mistakes during the game because she had tension as her thoughts were constantly circling on **"I must win" and "what if I fail**?"

Fear usually shoots out from bitterness due to unfolding of unknown future events. It gradually increases as you come across problems and failures while discharging responsibilities as adults. Apprehensions and panic in a way are also well knitted in your mind by past unfavourable events and situations. It is said that fear occurs due to a gene called 'stathmin' which may work on 'amygdala' in our brain which processes emotions including fear. I feel fear is also directly proportionate to your attachment levels-**The greater the attachment, the more the fear of losing it.** Take a look at the following brief real action-packed story of a dare devil mountaineer who fought fear of failure and in the process lost his arm. This story was subject of film, "127 Hours" released in 2010 and a book, "Between a Rock and a Hard Place."

Aron Ralston after travelling miles through the Utah (USA) canyons unfortunately found himself fallen into a gap with a rock trapping his arm. There was no way to move the rock as he was all alone and it soon became a life or death situation. He spent five full days overcoming hunger, thirst, mental breakdowns and physical pain. After examining each supply he had in his climbing bag, he attempted each one together and separate to help free his arm. He tried things that seemed impossible just to eliminate the 1% chance that it might work. When most people would quit, he never gave up. He tried chiselling a giant rock with a dull knife to using ropes as a pulley to try and get the rock to move. Aron ran out of food and water and was completely exhausted. Assuming that he would die, he spent five days slowly sipping his small amount of remaining water while trying to extricate his arm from the 800 pound rock but failed. After three days of trying to lift and break the rock, Aron prepared to amputate his trapped right arm at a point on the mid-forearm, in order to escape. He experimented with tourniquets and made some exploratory superficial cuts to his forearm in the first few days. On the fourth day, he realised that in order to free the arm he would have to cut through his bones, but he had insufficient tools to do so. When he ran out of water on the fifth day, he carved his name, date of birth and presumed date of death into the sandstone canyon wall, and videotaped his last goodbyes to his family. He did not expect to survive that night. He found himself still alive at the dawn of the following day. Aron walked out of that cave with one arm and attempted the 8-mile trek back to his car, a journey that would likely kill 98 percent of people. He was luckily saved a few miles out by some other climbers. (Excerpts: *wikipedia.org*)

I no way recommend what Aron did. It is an extreme step. It has been included as an example to show how some people are so daredevil that they are prepared to sacrifice even their body while taking their fears of failure head on. If the fear of failure had struck Thomas Edison, who knows we would still be in the age of candlelight and lanterns. Jack Welch, Bill Gates, Richard Branson, Donald Trump, Steve Jobs, Sam Walton, Rattan Tata, Narayan Murthi, etc. and several others will always be remembered for their fearless business leadership in spite of stiff opposition. They motivated and inspired thousands whose attempts to succeed didn't materialise in the first go.

I feel both failures as also the successful have fears. The failures have a fear whether they would succeed next time, public perception and that their competitors have gone ahead. While the successful fear for sustaining their achievements, peer competition and continued rise in expectations. In essence, your fears are responsible for both internal and external conflicts. This is all in mind and sooner you handle these imaginary negative feelings, the chances of success are enhanced. For example, many athletes and sportspersons some time perform under pressure because of high expectations from their fans, which often turns to fear. Take a look at the following interesting story:-

A little mouse was in constant fear of a cat that lived in the village. One day a powerful magician came to town. "My lord," "my life is miserable because of a cat. Why don't you make me into a cat? Then I would no longer live in fear." The magician used his wand, and the mouse found himself as a cat. But now a dog made his life unbearable with fear. The cat, desperate with fear, went back to the magician. "My lord," he said, "being a cat is most miserable because of a dog. Why don't you make me a dog? Then I would no longer live in fear." The magician obliged, and the cat became a dog. But he became a dog that lived in constant fear as there was a tiger living in the near by forest and made his life...miserable. Again, this poor creature set out for the magician. This time he asked to be made into a tiger, and it was done. Suddenly, the tiger found himself in constant threat from hunters. He had never known more fear than he did now. Finally, the magician was asked by the tiger to be made into a man, that he would fear nothing from that day on. For the first time, the magician spoke. ***"No physical form will rid you of fear, because there is no fear, it is in your imaginative mind and that is not in my control. No, I will not make you a man, I will again make you a mouse, for in your heart and you are a mouse anyway."***

Moral

When you fear, you become your own enemy and end up being a mouse whole life.

Fear not only leads to worry but it mentally cripples and you start becoming physically weak. It wipes out your dreams and makes you think twice before moving ahead on your success campaign. Just ponder over whether you can live a satisfying life and concentrate on your success campaign if you waste your time and energy focusing too much on "what and ifs." At times while working on your goal, suddenly your mind and thoughts traverse to the outcome of your efforts. All sorts of negative imaginary thoughts arise such as, "If I fail what will happen?" How can you work on your success campaign if you are constantly under the scanner of fear? Wouldn't it be better to focus on taking steps to minimise the fear by understanding that change always appears risky to begin with? Don't forget that all scientific discoveries and inventions have been a result of dedication, hard work and fearless fighting for years together. In the pursuit of inventions and innovations, there have been several failures. Those who persisted with their resolve and left behind fear, they emerged successful and got themselves registered in the hall of discovery and fame. Michael Jordan, the great Olympian once said, **"Obstacles don't have to stop you. If you run into a wall, don't turn around and give up. Figure out how to climb it, go through it, or work around it."**

Guidelines to Control Fear of Failure

Remember fear of failure keeps you saddled between 'should I or should I not' and consequently, you get stuck in situations you hate to be in. Whenever you decide to take the fear head on by facing and accepting it, you initiate positive steps to remove apprehensions and doubts about accomplishing your success campaign. Rarely one can find individuals who have the courage not to fear the failure. If you garner a mind-set that, **"whatever I undertake in life, there are chances of failure as there are for success,"** you move ahead with a relatively free mind. If you try to be utmost careful, walk sideways while working on your success campaign, there is a danger of disrupting your growth and development. For instance, Jeremy Bloom 29, a three-time world champion freestyle skier has mastered fear of failure. He once said that, "I look at [failures] as setbacks -- and I love setbacks because I think every setback gives you an opportunity to separate from everyone else. ... I love the challenges of those setbacks, and the opportunities that they present."

1. Break the imaginary glass partition

Breaking through the imaginary glass partition of fear is difficult unless you are able to brainwash your set beliefs, feelings and self-generate positive sentiments. It also happens that sometimes you initiate actions half heartedly since you are little enthusiastic to work on your goal and the moment you come across some hurdle, the imaginary glass partition of fear, doubt and apprehensions get reactivated. At times frustrated, you self -talk: "It is too difficult. I can't achieve it" "If

I fail, I will lose whatever I am doing" etc. This befits the saying that, **"When you doubt your power, you give power to your doubts."** This is the hour of trial and test of self-confidence. Showing your tail only pushes you away. As you gain experience in handling crisis situations, self- assurance will grow and the imaginary glass partition of doubt, uncertainty and fear will gradually diminish from your mind.

2. Face the fear head on

As said earlier, learn to accept that both failure and success are transitory. For example, if you receive a call from your CEO to meet him urgently, you may initially feel panicky and pressurised. You need to control your emotions and tune your mind to the subject of proposed discussions and quickly prepare yourself mentally by building on your self-belief. Look at children, they try and explore new things because they are yet to develop that sense of fear. But as they grow, the nuances of fear also take space in their mind and they forget to awake that fearless child in them which was exploring all the time. As said earlier, **fear can be defeated with courage and developing the right mind-set. Try to learn not to be cowed down by the consequences of failure. I am not advocating driving a car without the brakes or doing what Aron Ralston, the dare devil mountaineer did.** While taking fear head on, you need to be cautious and calculative. Never stop taking action in the right direction because it is the key component of your success campaign.

3. Security, comfort and fear is all in the mind

You may often feel that "I am secured at where I am and whatever I am doing." Most of you do not realise that security, comfort and fear are all in your mind psyche. For example, recall initial failed attempts to horse riding and the moment you were made to sit on the horse, fear was all that you were concentrating on. The moment fear started receding, you started enjoying the ride. Similarly, just before appearing in the examinations, you may always shiver with fear but the moment you start answering questions, your fear gradually disappears. Over the years, haven't you matured enough to overlook such imaginary fears and live a satisfied life? Did the people of Haiti know that a disaster was awaiting them? Most were inside their homes, yet they were not secured and safe. Life is dynamic, changing and risk prone no matter what you may do. Why fear when you know that evolving and dissolving is not in your hands. It is purely 'His' grace.

4. Analysing the fear

If you have a hard look at your life, you may come up with few instances/work related problems that you feared most. Can you trace their origin and analyse step by step to pinpoint the problem. Mostly you are well aware about what needs to be done. But you don't want to initiate steps to change because that involves taking risk. You may fail once or twice, but ultimately, you will succeed in controlling fear to a large extent. Can you spend some time in assessing potential results of your action before embarking on your next move? For example, suppose you know that you're afraid of speaking in public or afraid of making presentations to your senior management at work for fear of uttering something wrong. The best way is to make mock presentations before your friends and colleagues. Learn from mistakes by repeated practice before finally giving presentation to the senior management. It takes really one good performance and rest becomes history.

> *In 1979, I went to US on an international fellowship programme. I was one day asked to address a large gathering of Americans on 'India' in the evening. This was supposed to be the first such large interaction for which I was not prepared. I was compounded with fear the whole day. When I started speaking about India, I was nervous of performing in a foreign land and that too, before a large elite gathering. Initially, I fumbled as I was answering and attending to questions. One gentleman in the gathering criticised Late Indira Gandhi, former Prime Minister of India, while another one was critical of India's first nuclear explosion conducted successfully during 1974. O*

gosh! This build power and confidence in me and I started answering questions on a wide variety of subjects without any fear. Certain amount of aggressiveness got developed and my face was blushing with confidence and command. That was one important encounter of marching on fear fearlessly. (*Author's personal experience.*)

5. Take small jumps

Ask self, "What is the worst that could happen?" At best, "I will fail but I would continue to survive and live to try again." Lack of self-reliance and optimism even before initiating a change is bound to create fears and these result in unenthusiastic thoughts and low self-esteem. How about overcoming fear by taking small jumps rather than jumping by 'leaps and bounds.' As they say, **'Don't jump into water if you can't swim, but start getting your ankles wet.'** Break the fear related activities into small manageable parts and start working on these one by one. For example, if you fear group interaction, start practising by speaking before a mirror at home for couple of days. Follow it by making eye contact when meeting people and exchange pleasantries, such as hi, smile, etc. Next, initiate meeting with one or two individuals. Build on confidence by initiating discussion and putting your point of view, listening to theirs, etc. Once you feel confident, try interacting with a larger group.

6. Realistic expectations and outcome

Be doubly sure of expectations. There is an old saying, 'There is a slip between the cup and the lip'. Get wiser from this saying. It is advisable to prepare yourselves in advance for any possible occurrence or unexpected happenings. For example, starting with the 2008 economic melt down, many highfliers working for some top notch consulting companies in the US like Arthur Anderson, Merrill Lynch, etc. were not able to cope with realities and developed lot of fears pertaining to their performance and career prospects. Their expectations from the organisations, perhaps were high flying and not realistic.

7. Ignore negative influencers

It is important to associate with believers and achievers and not with negative and coward people. Bouncing back in life is no doubt a solo performance, but one needs emotional support and motivation from family, friends and superiors at work. Such support does wonders in stabilising your emotions, feelings and reducing mental tensions generally associated with attaining achievements in life.

8. Fear as an opportunity

As said earlier, try identifying issues and situations that make you fearful and panicky. There may be circumstances that you know little about or have never experienced or understood. Even ignorance of concerns at times leads to fear. Imagine these situations based on past experiences of failure or have a chat with others who have achieved success in the recent past. Concentrating and discussing fear related concerns in advance help to reduce panic and scare, and slowly turn to an opportunity to learn and grow. Jim Morrison, a renowned American poet and singer put it aptly when he said, "Expose yourself to your deepest fear; after that, fear has no power and the fear of freedom shrinks and vanishes. You are free." Remember the good old saying that, **"we can't discover new oceans unless we have the courage to leave the shore."** Take a lesson from the fact that, boats are safe at the river bank, but these are not made to be stay put at the river banks but cruise.

9. Overcome unconstructive thinking

Instead of filling your head with negative thoughts that will cause doubt and fear, fill it with optimism and hope. Keep repeatedly thinking and applying your mind to the fact that, "if others can fearless attain their accomplishments, why can't I?" Ultimately, what helps is stabilising your feelings by repeated practice.

Failure – An Opportunity in Learning

Right through school, college and then on to job, there is always emphasis on **doing it right the first time**. However, most people are rarely encouraged if they have a personal failure or commit mistakes on the job and nor are they given a chance to *learn* from failures to improve. What generally one hears is that we have failed to accomplish our objective and are unsuccessful. Learning from mistakes is a step towards self-development. On the contrary, when people accomplish their goals, they are often told that they were good and not just the rut of the mill. Committing mistakes undoubtedly leads to unbearable disappointments, but those who learn from each letdown become wiser and sooner get back to their success track with a resounding self-belief. To be honest, accepting mistakes and letdowns is a sign of maturity, transparency and learning. In the pursuit of your success campaign, there is no guarantee that you will succeed, you may even fail in spite of putting in your best. Never mind, you have an opportunity to learn from your mistakes, make amends in action, adjust the performance parameters and ultimately work with zeal to accomplish the campaign.

On a recent failure or underperformance, did you make self-assessment to measure your mistakes and make a note of these? Did you seriously concentrate and work on these and ensure their non-repetition? What did you do in case some of your actions didn't produce results? Did you try new ideas and options only if you are sure of your success? Do you attempt to immediately forget your failures? The answers to these and similar questions are preamble to your learning from failure. When you fail, you are told to go back and try again harder. This 'try again' connotes that you need to re-equip yourself by repeated trial and error and experimentation to revamp your skills and learn from mistakes before you restart your campaign again. Thomas Edison once wrote that **genius is 1% inspiration, 99% perspiration.** This perspiration is an outcome of learning on a failure. But as it is said that, **"If you're not making mistakes, you're not trying hard enough."** No learning is possible unless you are brave enough to have enough patience to experience and tolerate your mistakes and fallings, make appropriate amends and move on with your resolute.

Learning from failure is only possible if you are honest, serious and have an urge to pick the right reins. Moreover you are mentally tuned and prepared to bring in required changes in your thinking, attitudes, approach and willing to seriously work on carrying corrections and then rework. It seems difficult initially but as you start working, the process becomes easy and you start gaining confidence and comfort. Heavyweight boxer Muhammad Ali once said that, **"when a fighter doesn't get back up after being knocked down he forfeits any possible chance of winning the fight."** Many successful individuals, great leaders, famous sportspersons kept stock of important mistakes on their failures and would remember these every time they went on the success cruise. These great souls had developed a high forbearance for failure because they knew that each failure will chisel their skills for excellence in their campaign. AJ Lafley, former President and CEO of Procter & Gamble says that, **"most important and insightful learning is far more likely to come from failures than from success. Learning needs to be institutionalised to endure, otherwise you keep making the same mistake over and over and you don't learn from them."**

History is filled with organizations that failed in the initial years of existence with their product line or service.

But they regrouped, went back to the drawing board, R&D laboratory, reassessed and came up with what consumers were looking for. For instance, Hewlett-Packard's market share and profits went down during mid-1990s due to changing market scenario, strong competition and the growth of its computer business. HP hired Carly Fiorina to lead the company, who focussed on change of strategy, leadership and acquisition of Compaq. Her USP was adaptability and flexibility in handling change. It is said that Google Inc., suffered few setbacks since it went into business in the late 1990s and succeeded by studying the failures of other companies in order to help it innovate its technology and business model. Fred Smith, founder of Federal Express while studying at the Yale University received a C for his project outlining his vision for an overnight delivery service. When he actually carried out his "C" project to execution, FedEx became first overnight express delivery company in the world and the largest in the US. FedEx is a multi-billion dollar company today. NASA's space shuttle and ISRO's space programmes have learnt from failures and upgraded their performances which were subsequently reflected. Honda's learning through experimentation, trial and error continues to remain its hallmark. The company has made fantastic achievements after learning from scores of failures across. Honda employees say that, **"We can only make fantastic advances in technology through many failures."** But there are also instances where organizations didn't learn from mistakes and ultimately collapsed. For example, Eastern Airlines in the US came up with the promise of "Earn its Wings Everyday" by providing superior customer service, but at the same time losing passenger bags, flight cancellations/postponements/delays, etc. led to losing trust of customers and eventually, customers shifted to other airlines. The airline's employees failed to align their behaviour with the brand promise. Take a look at some more examples:-

- *Levi Strauss headed for the gold mines in California in the hope of finding gold. But he found none. Instead this failure gave him new knowledge of a gap in the marketplace. He began selling pants out of canvas for the miners which became a grand success. Today every one knows of Levi Strauss jeans.*

- *Honda Motor Company reinvented and brought out a range of high powered bikes that became very popular in the US after failing to market low-powered motorcycles that were popular in the suburbs of Tokyo.*
- *American author Mike Malone says that, 'Outsiders think of Silicon Valley as a success, but it is, in truth, a graveyard. Failure is Silicon Valley's greatest strength. Every failed product or enterprise is a lesson stored in the collective memory.* ***We don't stigmatise failure; we admire it. Venture Capitalists like to see a little failure in the résumés of entrepreneurs.'***
- *Thomas Watson, founder of IBM, once asked to see a recently promoted vice president who had failed on his first assignment in the new job, a mistake that cost the company a million dollars. The young man reported to the IBM chief prepared for the worst. "I guess you called me in to fire me," he said on entering Watson's office "Fire you!" exclaimed Watson, "We just spent $1,000,000 as part of your education!"*

Former US President Nixon once said, **"You must never be satisfied with success and you should never be discouraged by failure. Failure can be sad, but the greatest sadness is not to try and fail, but to fail to try."**

Take a look:-

A scientist was asked by a reporter how he was different from others. The scientist said that it all came from an experience when he was about two years old. He was trying to remove a bottle of milk from the refrigerator when he lost his grip and the bottle fell, spilling milk all over the kitchen. When his mother came, instead of yelling at him, she said, "Robert, what a great mess you have made! I have rarely seen such a huge puddle of milk. Well, the damage has already been done. Would you like to get down and play with the milk for a few minutes before we clean it up?" Indeed, he did. After a few minutes, his mother said, "You know, Robert, whenever you make a mess like this, eventually, you have to clean it up and restore everything to its proper order. So, how would you like to do that? We could use a sponge, a towel, or a mop. What do you prefer?" He chose the sponge and together they cleaned up the spilled milk. His mother then said, "You know, what we have here is a failed experiment in how to effectively carry a big milk bottle with two tiny hands. Let's go out in the backyard and fill the bottle with water and see if you can discover a way to carry it without dropping it."

The little boy learnt that if he grasped the bottle at the top near the lip with both hands, he could carry it without dropping it. The scientist then remarked that it was at that moment that he knew he didn't need to be afraid to make mistakes. Instead, he learnt that mistakes were just opportunities for learning something new, which is what scientific experiments are all about. George Bernard Shaw put it best, **"A life spent making mistakes is not only more honourable, but more useful than a life spent doing nothing."**

Learning from mistakes and carrying corrections is no doubt victory of keenness and zeal and without it, accomplishing your challenges will always appear like trekking Himalayas. No matter how fearsome and formidable the challenges look, without passion you would continue to live an ordinary life of 'as is where is'. Stanford University psychologist Carol Dweck has been studying how people handle failure for forty years. Based on her research, she identifies two distinct mind-sets that influence how we react to it. A fixed mind-set is based on the foundation that talent is genetic and it's entitled to success without much effort and regards failure as a personal affront. On the other hand, a growth mind-set assumes that no talent is entirely God gifted and that effort and learning makes everything possible. She sees failure as an opportunity and not a disgrace. When a growth mind-set is challenged, it's quick to reassess, adjust and try again. According to Dweck, parents and teachers often push children into fixed mind-sets by rewarding certain behaviours and misdirecting praise. "Talent isn't passed down in the genes; it's passed down in the mind-set." (Ref: Mindset: The New Psychology of Success by Dweck). Audrey Hunt, a personal friend of mine and a well-known music teacher in the US whose students have appeared on Broadway in New York and American Idol shares her thoughts on learning as given below:

> *"I have learned through the years that for me failure does not exist. Learning opportunities come in various forms – the greatest being failure. If we think we have failed at something, bless that experience and give thanks for another way to learn and grow. Do I wish I could have done better in the past? Sure I do. However, I am where I am because of past choices. As long as I love who and what I am, I create peace and harmony for myself."*

US General William Westmoreland was once reviewing a platoon of paratroopers in Vietnam. As he went down the line, he asked each of them a question: "How do you like jumping, son?" "Love it, sir!" was the first answer. "How do you like jumping?" he asked the next. "The greatest experience in my life, sir!" exclaimed the paratrooper. **"How do you like jumping?" he asked the third. "I hate it sir." "Then why do you do it?" "I want to be around guys who love to jump?"**

I was highly impressed to read about D.J. Gregory, an American who started his life journey with challenges-born with cerebral palsy, underdeveloped lungs and his legs entangled. Despite his cerebral palsy, he has extreme passion for playing golf. His game is not perfect but keeps striving time and again to be among best. He says, **"If you have a dream go after it. Don't let anybody tell you that you can't do something. You get back up and you learn from your mistakes and you don't do it again."** Gregory is an outstanding example of learning from failure.

Guidelines to Learning from Failure

You often hear teachers or bosses having inclination for people development, say experience is the best teacher. You need to accept failure as one of the many lessons you gain from experience. Your learning initiative requires rewinding to assess drawbacks and snags in your earlier campaign. Be prepared to act on what others advise you even if you do not like what you hear. While working in the organizations, it is a general trend that individuals are punished for committing mistakes rather than being encouraged because it is perceived that mistakes cost money and time. Individuals thus are found reluctant to admit weaknesses and mistakes. You may have to live with such experiences sometimes.

- As said earlier, *look at the mistakes in-depth,* identify the main causes and find why did you fail? What were the factors responsible? Where did things go hay way? Deliberate whether you could think of new ideas and look at your limitations if any? Evaluate alternative approaches to strike back. Michael Johnson says that, **"You learn as much from those who have failed as from those who have succeeded."** It would be advisable to divide the cause and reason into small parts and take each part separately and do an in-depth analysis of reasons and find the solution to overcome. For instance, the goal set for achieving may have not been specific or it was not realistic or you were not fully geared up to work and accomplish it. Sit quietly in a place undisturbed and think how you could overcome the problem and what all you are prepared to sacrifice in the process of learning. Tweeting through following questions might help:

    1. Specific causes and reasons that led to failure. What are the specific concerns that need to be put under scanner?
    2. What are the focal points of learning and how you plan to do that? How is your

approach on the success campaign going to be different next time?

- Failure is a mechanism and opportunity for revival, the more you try to learn from mistakes, the better are your chances to succeed next time. When you were young, you experimented and explored the unknown world around you by trying new things and learn from what happens. Recall how you learnt participating in track events in school. You had number of falls and mistakes, rectified these and ultimately succeeded in bringing laurels to your school-house. Learn how to be better prepared not only to expect to deal with some failure, but to be better able to deal with mistakes in future as well. Colin Powell said once that, **"There are no secrets to success. It is the result of preparation, hard work, and learning from failure."**
- While learning from failures or mistakes, you may have negative emotions as to why you failed and this thought is going to disturb your learning process. Remember no fruitful learning will take place unless you have stable feelings and leave behind the outcome of your earlier attempt, and instead concentrate on how to improve to make it this time. You will increase your learning when you are able to manage your feelings by recovering from it quickly. You not only learn from failure about your potential and weak areas, but also self-develop from the experience.
- What separates winners from failures is the ability to rise above losing by learning from the experience. Many great success stories will tell you how tables were turned immediately after failure by individuals by carrying in-depth self-assessment and being desperate and persistent with their goals. Having learnt from past experiences, **get, set and go and try again**. You are very well aware what Great Napoleon said once

that, **"a winner never quits and a quitter never wins."** A Winner never quits why? Because he keeps trying and learning from the experiences gained out of each attempt.

- By nature, most do not easily admit their mistakes, an outcome of false ego. An early admission helps avert bigger hardships ahead because the learning process essentially is an initiative to evaluate, accept and rectify the mistakes.
- Learning from failure cannot happen overnight; it requires patience, tolerating frustrations and pressures to perform, plan for improvement, resolve.
- Often on a consistent record of success, you don't learn many aspects of handling hardships in life- a must for smooth ride. No doubt one learns from successes as well, but there appears to be a limitation because one often gets carried away. I have always felt that, **unless we taste sourness, we can't relish sweetness.**
- Learning through self-development is passion and a self-initiative. You need to create an inner urge, drive and will to learn. Looking at a mistake and rectifying it is a temporary solution. Carry repeated practice to change habits, attitudes and beliefs to alter your behaviour. You may like to take help of your friends/colleagues/boss for advice and training. An outside perspective on your behaviour will be more objective than your own.
- Failure has constructive messages hidden. It alerts to your mistakes and sometimes throws light on some unexpected opportunities hidden in it. **Recall as a child you fell several times, while playing with children. What did you do?** You jumped back unmindful of dusting your clothes and refocussed on playing and not letting the fall stop you. Bring out the child within by picking and dusting yourself and start all over again by not giving failure a second thought. Try to be familiar with these experiences as

learning opportunities and don't hide these away out of fear and humiliation.

To sum up, we all have blind spots. The difference lies in whether we are focussed on these to improve or carry these as it is. Samuel Smiles, a Scottish and author of famous treatise, 'Self Help' said, "We learn wisdom from failure much more than from success. We often discover what will do, by finding out what will not do; and probably, he who never made a mistake never made a discovery." On accomplishing your success campaign when you look back, you would realise that had you not failed, you would have remained aloof from gaining valuable experiences out of learning. Success then appears like being on the top of Mount Everest. What are needed are your perseverance and an open mind to learn from failures and mistakes, implementing learning and changing yourself to being a highly successful individual.

How to Handle Stress on a Failure

Failure to accomplish your success campaign or inability to handle an assignment or the prospect of competing with someone you perceived as more capable, etc. is no doubt fearsome and worrisome and sooner, it makes you stressful and traumatic. Stress is the physical and mental response of your body to demands made upon it. It is the result of your reaction to outside events, not necessarily, the events themselves. This adds to your woes and locks away the mental strain. While some stress is a usual part of wear and tear on a failure, excessive stress can interfere with your success campaign of rebuilding from ground zero and reduce your physical and emotional health. Feeling besieged with negative thoughts and imaginary outcome of failure not only makes you lose confidence and willpower, but also makes you withdrawn and slowly starts affecting your overall well-being. It is reported that a recent survey of American workers revealed that, 80 percent of employees felt the previous year was their most stressful year ever at work. Symptoms of stress are: Feeling anxious, irritable, depressed, loss of interest in work, lack of concentration, social withdrawal, anxiety to perform, public perception, loss of sleep and appetite, low self-esteem, anger, panic attacks, phobias, sexual dysfunction, depression and problems with interpersonal relationships, etc. When you are continuously stressed out and feel anxious off and on, you enter a phase where likelihood of getting into depression mode increase and it is difficult to realise before stress turns into a 'mental health problem'. According to WHO reports, 36 percent of Indians today suffer from some form of depression or the other and by 2020, depression will assume alarming proportion world over and will be next only to heart diseases. Medical researchers estimate that between 50 and 70 percent of disease and illness are in part due to long-term stress. Experiencing stress varies from people to people based on their personality dynamics and coping strength. There can be instances where one person may exhibit a total sense of stress, nervousness and frustration, while another person may feel calm and composed.

Guidelines to Managing Stress

1. Assess opinions and views

You are rarely sensitive to power of your thoughts that can inflict deep emotional hurt or generate aura around. If your thoughts are optimistic and encouraging, these attract helpful circumstances and opportunities in your life. On the contrary, if you have negative connotations in life, you would see the negative in every aspect of life including positive ones. Thinking about past drains, most of your mind energy while thinking about future leads to the feeling of panic and doubt which leads to depressing energy. No matter whatever is the outcome of your campaign, the practice of being confident not only keeps the determination and will to fight alive, but it also helps to play down the unenthusiastic events and continue focussing on the campaign. Many things in life are beyond your control— particularly, the behaviour of other people. Rather than stressing out over them, focus on the things you can control, such as the way you choose to react to problems. Work towards your success campaign as hard as possible and be prepared to accept whatever is the result. I know it is easy said difficult done, but you need to learn and nurture this habit in the interest of keeping stress away. Remember, **you can achieve anything in life provided your body and mind is stress free as far as possible. What can a stressful mind achieve –**

nothing really except pollute the immediate surroundings of people with the bad aura? (For details, see chapter 13.)

2. Control feelings

Common emotional effects out of stress are: impatience, anger, frustration, fear, anxiety, feelings of inadequacy, insecurity and depression. When stress is accompanied by anger, you may become less tolerant. According to psychological studies, people with high level of emotional instability do not handle stress well. They are often moody, anxious and uncomfortable, and have a tendency towards negative thinking. Controlling emotions calls for developing a high level of self-assurance and habit of moving ahead by not keep beating about the bush repeatedly.

3. Personality dynamics

Your personality characteristics are no doubt patterned at birth and may also be genetic, but you have the power to mould these to betterment by repeated practice. For example, some of you are too sensitive and have knee-jerk reaction to stress and often feel negative on the spur of moment than others who remain relatively calm, unfazed and take problems in stride. Temperaments can be altered by changing your conduct, habits and tuning your mind to be open and flexible. Reactions can be minimised and changes incorporated by practice and focussed efforts. Learn from athletes who lose several times, yet keep a calm mind and try their best to beat the competition.

4. Be internalised

At times, failure may appear like being in the deep sea surrounded by sharks, snakes, and other aquatic animals waiting eagerly to hunt you down. Whether success or failure, you would continue to be surrounded by some people with habits similar to those of sharks, snakes and scorpions, etc. Such people are found depicting their sympathies more for public consumption while beneath nice postures, they carry malice and look for an earliest opportunity to hit you below the belt. Their behaviour at times appear somewhat like sharks hunting with little conscience and you need to be smart enough to stay as far away as possible. By nature you tend to externalise your expressions for social comparisons, building your equity in the public domain and power. This makes you prone to depression, despair and hopelessness. While maintaining external manifestations, try initiating a process of internalising so that you have more control on your situations and are relatively free to decide what you want to do.

5. Avoid social comparisons

Get out of the habit of social comparisons and understand that each one is unique and has different dreams and carved ones own journey. Some are lucky enough to walk the journey fast without any hiccups. While for some, the journey may be tedious. Let you focus on your own journey. Focussing on other's journey brings in mental strain.

6. Failures and Mistakes are as much part of Life as Love, Hate and Anger

In the unfortunate event of repeated failures, there is a possibility of close friends and colleagues slowly starting to give cold shoulders. It is only few of your close family members who remain at your beck and call and keep exciting. They are as much worried on your repeated failures as you yourself are. This is the real time to learn vagaries and impulses of some phases of life and also study the flux of human mind, a chance that most successful remain detached from learning. Nevertheless, your response to such behaviour lies in not being disheartened, discouraged, angry, reactive, and unhappy, but being anxious in performing and turning the tables. There are also occasions in life when while climbing the success ladder, you make people jealous or unintentionally step on their toes. People don't forgive but wait for an earliest opportunity to take revenge. For example, a sea shell looks elegant from exterior, but it is full of dirt inside. Ironically, the same people have an opaque and non-transparent mind. Your acute urge and pushiness backed by self-assurance to strike at success is not only 'survival of the fittest' but a befitting reply to all those who try to install fear and make mockery of failure.

There may be also occasions when you fail and the co-competitors succeed and you may feel like a fish out of water. Don't wait, get back to water and try to swim faster and better and prove the mantle. Someone has rightly advocated that, **"There are those who make things happen, those watch things happen, and those who wonder what happened."** Life keeps changing so does your process to tackle each situation. Can you try and be one among those, who go all out to make things happen and leave others to wonder what really happened? An African proverb beautifully sums up, **"A calm sea does not make a skilled sailor."** Sometimes, you may come across individuals doing very well in life and boosting about their unblemished success record and power to demoralise people around and through their tantrums. I feel this is absurd, myth, a self-generated publicity gimmick, and prophesy. Don't get discouraged by their broad smile or flamboyant character, some of them may be broken inside and having sleepless nights. Admitting failure is a sign of maturity, openness and confidence. Very rarely, I have seen people admitting to their failure irrespective of their successful status. They are the ones who are the real weak and meek and in case of a small failure, would be the first one to crash on the bed and hide their head under a quilt.

7. Why feel humiliated

There are hundreds of experiences of humiliation one undergoes in life – both within and outside the organization. Humiliations of late have started becoming part of our way of life and depict our dirty mental make up with no control on unconstructive feelings. Those who humiliate are only giving dent to their frustrations and depict their obnoxious behaviour. Some people are rarely sensitive to use humiliation privately as a tool for reprimand and development. Why can't they learn from Nature? When an avalanche takes place in the higher regions of mountains, there is no one to watch except may be a crow. Some are so thick-skinned; it really does not bother them. They are rarely sensitive and feel it is part of life, carry on unaffected with their lives and often succeed in achieving their goals. There are others who have intense feelings. This leads them to a sense of embarrassment and humiliation. For them, it is like **'swimming with the sharks'**. Humiliation may also be caused by feelings of guilt and at times leads you to withdraw. If you happen to make a mistake, you don't have to tell yourself that you have failed. Omissions, miscalculations, wrong choices etc. are part of life. Humiliations, insults, feeling of let down, and shame can occur at any time in any way irrespective whether you are successful or failure. As they say 'every action in life produces reaction-good or bad'. **At times the feeling of humiliation is more in individuals who have higher levels of ego, self-esteem, and more worried about protecting their self-image**. Success is not a license against humiliations. Every successful individual faces mistakes, defeats, humiliations, tragedies and failures. Laurence Shames puts it beautifully, **"Success and failure. We think of them as opposites, but they're really companions - the hero and the sidekick."** Humiliation is like an earthquake, one doesn't know when it will happen. You have to be mentally prepared for an unforseen eventuality. Remember whenever and wherever humiliation gives you a kick, turn this kick to your advantage to move forward and not get bogged down with stress and low feelings.

8. Stress busters

Self-healing: Self-healing through meditation not only cleanses unwanted thoughts and reactions from your mind, but helps improve emotional and physical well-being. Close the eyes and slowly take a deep breath. In order to concentrate, focus the mind on some symbol/object/breathing. The body needs to be put at complete rest with no part/muscle being tight. Distractions will play seek and hide with your mind. But continue focussing on the object you are concentrating on.

Breathing: Breathing exercise is a mind de-stressor and regulates energy in the body. Take slowly deep breath in through your nose. Feel the air going in and try to expand the abdomen in wards as much as possible to reap better benefits of breathing. After a pause, exhale the stale air out slowly through nose only by squeesing the stomach.

Humour and laughter: This is a value chain in human system and is like the 'icing on the cake' and acts as a bridge to happiness, intimacy and togetherness. Humour and laughter in your life strengthens your immune system, boosts energy and reduces stress.

Practising emotional intelligence: Daniel Goleman's Emotional Intelligence (EI) is a technique for understanding, directing and managing emotions in positive ways. It helps to manage emotional variations by making you understand how your emotions influence your thoughts, actions and feelings. It gradually helps release these and the mental stress. EI is the ability to use your emotions in constructive ways by communicating with others in such a way that brings people close to you and overcomes differences by understanding others' feelings and being empathetic. It helps to de-stress by revamping your hurt feelings by self-awareness and improves self-confidence. Try practising the following skills:-

a) **Self-Awareness:** Knowing your feelings, realistic assessment of your abilities, strengths, limitations, self-confidence.

b) **Self-Regulation:** Emotions to facilitate rather interfere, keeping disruptive emotions and impulses in check, honesty and integrity, adaptability, flexibility in handling change.

c) **Motivation:** Preferences to take initiative and strive to have perseverance in case of setbacks, striving to improve, commitment.

d) **Empathy:** Sensing what others are feeling and being able to take their perspective and cultivating a rapport.
e) **Social skills:** Handle emotions in relationships by persuading, compensating and not competing, settling disputes/disagreements by co-operation and facilitation.

Share feelings: Often you are too good at suppressing feelings to keep up your image in the public domain. Actually, beneath your wail of satisfaction, you may be most depressed, dissatisfied and frustrated. Don't suppress feelings, but discuss and share to lessen the mental strain. Discussing stressful feelings with family or friends without their being judgemental helps ease some of the tension.

Have realistic goals: Achieving success at the cost of your health, i.e., keep working hard without adequate rest is an unrealistic goal that ultimately leads to pressures and anxiety. Researchers at the University of British Columbia, Vancouver and Concordia University, Montreal teamed up to investigate what happens when people set goals that they do not reach. They found that increased stress from unattained goals leads to elevated levels of CRP (C-reactive Protein), a biological measure of inflammation. Over time, chronic levels of inflammation heighten the risk of many diseases including diabetes, osteoporosis and heart diseases. Therefore, keep goals realistic and be flexible.

Have a healthy lifestyle: Living a healthy lifestyle by changing your habits on physical activity, food and relaxation often helps to beat stress and tension. For instance:

1. Releasing stress through exercise or physical activity such as brisk walk, jogging, playing games or carrying out other physical activities such as gardening, helping in household jobs not only activates your body muscles and joints but relaxes, keeps you fit and releases tension that deviates mind from offshoots of failure. Physical exercise is aiso effective in strengthening your body's resistance power.

2. Lack of sleep can be susceptible to stress. When your body and mind is well-rested, it helps to keep your mental-emotional balance and you are able to create and draw on your energy levels and recoup to work on your campaign. Should there be bout of stress during working on your success campaign, it is advisable to stop work and move out to take a stroll. Physical movement away from the scene of work not only detaches from the routine, but also helps to quickly reduce stress and may also give the opportunity to explore fresh creative ideas.
3. Try vigorously to stop smoking in case you happen to be a smoker, reduce intake of liquor, coffee and tea, beverages like soda, etc.

How to Cope up with Failure

Disappointments and distress on a failure keeps every one messed up, haunting and hurting till one is able to receive comfort, encouragement and sympathy from one's well-wishers. While it is essential to evaluate reasons of your failure, but at the same time, getting struck with these and keep thinking about it over and over again only adds to your woes. It is wiser to plan the future course of action, double the resolve and move on with your success campaign. Learning to cope up with failure in a professional way expects a great deal of self-discipline and controlled sentiments on your part. It is a self- driven process and a serious affair that needs full concentration, practice and being hopeful. As time passes and discontentment settles down, try understanding that yesterday was a different day, forget it as a bad dream and look for a bright and enthusiastic today. As beautifully enumerated by *Johnson, former US President that,* **"Yesterday is not ours to recover, but tomorrow is ours to win or lose."**

Coping Guidelines

How about treating failure as an opening that helps unfasten new panorama? Take a step back and look at the big picture without pre-conceived notions. While coping to some extent will help easing your apprehensions and fears, and give a new direction to your venture, yet in a highly competitive environment, the unmatched efforts may fall short of expectations for which you need to be prepared.

Failure does not mean you sit back, grumble and go into a shell. It is a challenge to re strategise your campaign with a motto -**Just Don't Give up!**

1. Taking a proactive approach

Most people take a reactive approach and end up disturbing their mind-set, get fuming and become anxious. Taking a proactive approach is a professional way of handling failure and coping with the afteraffects. This will not only help to transact well with each of the hurdles out of a failure, but also facilitate you to pull out from low motivation and move on.

2. Gathering feedback

It is important to gather feedback by listening to other's opinions, suggestions and experiences as also to assess your gut feel and intuition and work on these. Analyse the feedback and take corrective measures wherever possible. Feedback helps to perform in a different way next time and often this becomes a springboard to success.

3. Look for lessons

How you view your let down, descend and hold up will ultimately impact your rebuilding of success campaign. There are no doubt lessons to be learnt out of a failure, so identify these in a patient manner and make mental notes. As said earlier, assess, could you have concentrated more on your weaknesses? Do you need to revise your action plan? Would a different approach work? Focus on learning from what went wrong and then formulate a revised action plan, ensuring that there are no repetitions of mistakes and that you're better prepared to move on with the campaign.

4. Improve on tolerance levels

Patience is the ability to tolerate waiting and delay without becoming agitated or upset. It is a state of staying on power and signifies your elasticity and resolution. Learning and practising being tolerant and enduring helps in coping and gradually healing. Try looking at problems of delay or hurt from a larger perspective.

5. Don't blame others

Some of you are narrow, selfish and good at passing the fault. Blaming appears the easiest thing in the world to save skin till the truth is known. If your choice for options has turned wrong, why don't you accept it instead of blaming family, colleagues, luck or the system? Don't blame the circumstances; you are the one to be blamed in the first place for having created these. Passing the blame or making excuses may bring in temporary mental relief. Accept responsibility for failure and don't search for a scapegoat and blame an external factor. When you are in the middle of a river why blame the surging waters, high waves or even flood. Be bold and accept responsibility and steer the way to the best of your capability to cross the river. Even at work, a good manager is one who accepts his responsibility of action and not passes the buck on to the subordinates. The manager not only earns the trust and respect of the team, but also gets known as a person who leads from the front and not the one who often ducks, should there be an obstacle. By accepting the responsibility, you are not only meeting the failure head on but also maintaining your belief in self which is important for a re assault on the success campaign.

6. Feed the mind with positive and optimistic thoughts

Failure and letdowns do surround you with unconstructive thoughts, loss of interest in networking and a sense of hopelessness. In a state like this, coping becomes extremely difficult. Start feeding the mind with enthusiastic and cheerful thoughts by reading books, especially on famous failure-success stories, such as Walt Disney, Colonel Sanders, Richard Branson, Donald Trump, Dr. APJ Abdul Kalam etc. and reflect on their thoughts and get inspired. I was going through the interview of Anupam Kher, Bollywood actor who in spite of having appeared in nearly 400 films and 100 plays yet **has been through extreme struggles, ups and downs.** He says, "When I was a struggling actor, I survived on motivational lives and on autobiographies of Charlie Chaplin, Vincent Van Gogh, Mahatma Gandhi, Pandit Nehru, etc. I realised that these great people have also gone through so much, I'll make it one day. That kept me going."

7. Remember past performances

If you cast your mind to the immediate past, you will recall several successes you may have undergone in order to reach where you are today. Some success experiences will go a long way in restoring your self-confidence and recharging you.

8. Don't pity self

Never talk trash about self nor believe that you are no good. Instead keep faith in self, realise that one or two failures don't change your inherent strengths. This finds support from Mark Leary, Wake Forest University psychologist, who says that it is important to have self-compassion, the ability to treat oneself kindly on the face of failure, rejection, defeat and other negative events. Leary based on a research survey found that those with higher self-compassion were more likely to think, **"Everybody goofs up now and then" and less likely to think, "I am such a loser" or "I wish I could die."**

9. Pursue more than one goal

By having more than one expertise, the chances are that you will not be disappointed in life. If you don't click hundred percent in one profession, you can look at the alternative for survival. Pursuing more than one goal always helps to avoid the agony of failure and feeling of helplessness.

10. Socialise to harmonise

Spending time in social networking stabilises emotions and brings in positive change in your perspectives. Your family has a special role to play by ensuring that you remain motivated and encouraged to fight back. Relationships more often act as a driver of change and are a bridge that connects feelings, sentiments, builds trust and helps in social and professional success. Appreciate that family relationships usually stand by you no matter the relationships may have somewhat diluted with the passage of time. Reconnection with family roots is a life beyond niches and a ladder to a positive state of mind, stabilised feelings and thoughts. It is like a retreat that renews and energises your mind and body. Your spouse/ family are not only partners in progress but in failure as well.

11. Anticipate failures

Before restarting work on your success campaign, it is important to spend some time visualising and anticipating what kind of failures you may face ahead and what are your preparations to meet these to minimise hiccups and surprise elements. Identify personal gaps if any. Study the campaign from all perspectives, anticipating potential challenges and determining beforehand how you will respond to those challenges. From this perspective, you can quickly recognise which areas in your success campaign need special attention. Acting on right priorities today will enhance your preparedness to those priorities.

Part–3

Towards Stitching Success

Transform Self to Succeed in Life

Stitching up success is not possible unless you initiate certain amount of personal transformation to undertake the process of change that will surely be a new path, a new destination, a transition to your future development and growth. Naturally your understanding of personal transformation, its necessity and your response to changed situations become important. It is not required for only immediate gains, but it is a vehicle for long time betterment, both in professional and personal goals and moving beyond failure. I feel there are only two aspects in life which are permanent, viz. rising and setting of sun and process of transformation. **Rest everything is temporary – success and failure, rich and poor, healthy and sick, gain and loss, love and hate, night and day, etc**. If you understand this premise, it will be somewhat easy to accomplish your success campaign. Most of us are fearful of carrying personal transformation because we don't believe we have any control over how or when transformation happens to us. In his classics, 'Who Moved My Cheese,' author, Spencer Johnson depicts what matters most is the attitude one has to have about carrying transformation through change. It is important to understand that every one sooner or later is going to experience change in their lives. In fact, we change every moment, yet we don't realise it. Those of you who believe in change will sooner or later embrace success. However, should you remain static and behind, you are bound to fail in your success campaign.

Mikhail Gorbachev, the former president of erstwhile USSR once said, **"We are all products of our time. If change is to happen, we will have to change ourselves."** When you initiate a process of transformation, it may appear difficult to cope up and you might end up thinking that change as being contrary to your interest and not giving instant results. You therefore resist it because you feel it is risk taking and also countless negative thoughts occupy your mind. For example, how much discomfort initially you feel if there is a small change in your own personal or family settings? Your spouse/family takes the brunt of your reactions to a minor change? This is where success achievers score over failures by trying with the changed course of action, implementing new ideas and new methods to reach their goals. Carly Fiorina, former CEO of Hewlett Packard who was responsible for bringing Changes in H-P's culture and structure often quotes Charles Darwin: **"It is not the strongest of the species who survive, nor the most intelligent, but those who are most adaptive to change."**

From my personal experience and that of others, I know that personal transformation and incorporating changes in life usually are stressful, apprehensive though these are absolutely essential. No personal transformation will be successful unless there is motivation to change, desire to acquire new and renewed behaviour, possessing dedication, acceptance and an inner urge for accomplishing your success campaign. It is true that when circumstances are hard, you fail to understand or accept the role of modification in your lives. In fact, you may feel threatened and irritated if you are told to amend. It is only when mind is calm and emotions are stabilised, you feel the necessity to bring gradual change and tune your mind in that direction. Change is a direction, a revolution to learning new things and engaging in a diversity of panorama. Imagine if you were asked to hold a fist full of water tightly, the water will drain through your fingers. On the contrary, you can join both hands and try to hold water by staying still. This is change which is more of common sense, boldness, and self-experimenting rather than sitting cross-legged with hands folded and just mutely watch winners pass by.

Just Think!

- You frequently change relationships, jobs, brands and lifestyle, but when you are asked to change yourself, you resist as if you are signing your own death warrant?
- It is true that adapting to changed situations is an arduous task, but persistency makes it possible. Most of you have a common belief that nature and temperament can't be altered. But the fact is that attitudes and temperaments are definitely possible to be altered with constant practice and self-affirmations. When you fail or perform below expectations, you have no other alternative, but to change and try adjusting the mind to a new situation, revised and better methods of preparation/working/behavioural interactions, etc. It becomes easy since the ego levels often come down and adaptation becomes possible. What is inducted forcefully gradually becomes part of your conduct and personality.

Mikhail Gorbachev once beautifully summarised the essence of change, **"Revolution means construction but it also always implies demolition, without demolition you cannot clear the site for new construction."** What Gorbachev was advocating that, change can't succeed unless you are prepared to sacrifice your emotional attachments with power, people and old ways of doing work, thoughts, feelings, comfort zone, and habits? The transition of change does involve fear of unknown and worry. Can you attempt to answer honestly questions, such as: Whether your interpersonal behaviour, emotions, openness/closeness, relationships, etc. need to change to make you more people friendly, be with time, and acceptable? Whether you need to be more cooperative? How well-prepared and equipped are you to challenge success? What are your strengths and weaknesses in general and vis-a-vis your current purpose? How soon you get nervous and demoralised, should there be hurdles or underperformance, etc? Such or similar questions are extremely important for building a base for your success campaign with being high on self-pledge and credence. Changing your objectives of converting failure to success necessitates adaptation and adjustment with new situations, new people, new methods of working, etc. Adapt a gradual process of modification by taking help from friends who have undergone transformation in their overall behaviour, attitudes and habits.

Guidelines for Personal Transformation

On rebuilding from ground zero on a letdown, if you feel seriously certain aspects of your ways of handling challenges do really need deeper looking at, I feel you are already on the right track to accomplish your success campaign.

1. Self-assessment

Before embarking on your personal transformation, the first and foremost task is to evaluate the self, **analyse your past failures and reasons thereof. Assess** how you can prevent them in the future. Similarly analyse success in the recent past to regain some lost confidence levels. Having identified areas of concern for correction, you need to dispassionately apply your mind to think as to how you can go about carrying your personal transformation for change. Not an easy task, but requires patience and the will to change. Undertaking corrections and modifications do at times lead to experiencing temporary moments of anxiety and discomfort. At times it appears that all doors are closed and so are the roads leading to success. Remember that door to the natural process of adjustment to change is always open; it is for you to walk through the door and become stronger, mature, and forward-looking. (For details, see chapter 10.)

2. Studying mental-set up

Personal transformation is not possible unless your mind is in tune with accepting change. Not an easy task because minds are always sceptical, resistance-prone and are rarely in 'Now' in this moment. The most important change in your life is that of initiating and assessing of your attitudes and incorporating planned changes. Whether a glass is half full or half empty depends on your attitude. Often you may think in terms of managing obstructions to achieving success, but the approach usually is half-hearted. Making few changes here and there without going in little depth doesn't help. In order to breed affirmative mind energy for achieving success, you have to learn to try different routes to success, evolve new paths, new and revised thinking paradigms. For example, solving a mathematical puzzle has various alternatives. Similarly, for solving a business management case, there are empty numbers of alternatives. One is interested in a solution which is most effective and saves resources of a business enterprise. (For details, see chapter 13.)

3. Become self-conscious

Most people seem to be devoid of hearing out and understanding what their conscious is conveying. They seem to be in a hurry to achieve their objective by hook or crook. This may work for some time, but I feel this often entangles you as you move forward in life to handle bigger challenges. Therefore, develop the habit of listening to your consciousness, your inner voice. It often is the voice of change for betterment. It will also help you to decipher between choices available and what option would suit the best in a given circumstance.

4. Have a strong belief in the self

A strong belief in the self is undoubtedly the anchor for transformation. It is the master key. Therefore, work on your belief systems first and ensure that unconstructive leanings gradually vanish and you are able to slowly inculcate positive and constructive ideas about yourself, other people and your surroundings. Try transmitting your positive aura to your self frequently and you would gradually experience change to betterment and notice certain amount of enthusiasm in your stride as you walk with purpose and direction, and this will transmit on to your success campaign. When you feel secure and confident, you can make the task of the transition in a more productive way. (For details, see chapter 18.)

5. Initiate small changes to begin with

Transforming self to a changed thinking is like walking alone up the hill. It can take place any time, but often it may start with the change in life perspectives, meeting with learned individuals or due to a set back. Rarely people are found interested in personal transformation just because of their static mental programming. Even bringing little change by managing small resistances here and there and continue on the path of self-transformation will ultimately help in achieving success. Personal transformation is a continuous process, and it involves a great struggle with your ego levels, inflexible attitudes and beliefs engrained in you right through childhood. Try to counter these in a phased and planned manner by evaluating what is ultimately beneficial to you. Work hard on self-conduct and try to even bring a 5-10% change and never mind, if that happens over a period of time. Gradually, personal transformation becomes part of your personality dynamics and changed behavioural responses start emanating from your mind which are most often misunderstood and misread resulting in complications because of not being on the same page. For instance,

> *After getting separated from my last job, I did become demotivated and low, and the shock of losing a high paid job was unbearable. Slowly, I witnessed a self-change. I recall my children often telling me, "Papa where has your aggressiveness and zeal gone?" Apparently, they were not comfortable with observing change in me and felt that I was slowly turning weak due to failures. (Author's personal experience)*

I feel the only way out in these situations is to keep your changed conduct to yourselves and not go around propagating it and have the wrath of every one around. Secondly, if you convince people around with benefits of change, this may slowly start registering, but the moment they interact with others; there is a likelyhood of reverting to the earlier behaviour. I know some readers may not agree and try to put the realities under the carpet and continue spending life unchanged. I remember once I told an acquaintance about changing his vision and priorities in life. He shot back, "failures think that way. My dear grapes are sour." With a mind-set such as this, personal transformation is usually put at the back burner. The irony of the matter is that the same individual's day in and day out crib that their children don't change to a constructive behaviour.

6. Have self-acceptance

There is no doubt that modifying self is most arduous and causes some ripples, interference, sufferings and reservations (all in mind). Initiating change means breaking the shackles of status quo which often is not easy but can be achieved by your bendable and steadfast approach; firmness of purpose, constant practice and strength of character. Once you take a thrust, gradually, you learn to live with new and improvised behavioural transactions that not only open new vistas, but also unearth your vast potential which may have remained un-utilised.

7. Transformation internally raises fear and doubts

Handle personal transformation with care, drive and a positive approach. This is done by brainwashing the negatives in the subconscious mind, but that doesn't happen overnight. It takes lot of practice and certain amount of time. Cheerfulness is a platform for change and failures need to change statements, such as "It's a myth - thoughts never change," to "With control, self-affirmations and practice thoughts will change." Be contented and don't look around too much at the flashy exterior of people, it disturbs and creates obstacles in personal transformation. (For details, see chapter 12.)

Perform an Honest Self-Assessment

Once you are convinced and have mentally made up your mind to initiate personal transformation, the next important step is to wisely proceed to improve yourself by first carrying an honest self-assessment. It helps in identifying your pitfalls and weaknesses that become impediments in your earlier success pursue. What is within you is often best known to you and it is therefore important that self-assessment reflects your personal values, interests, personality traits and skills to help locate factors that were responsible for your failure and also act as an indicator to work on and improve. When we talk of self- development, it is basically being a self-change agent. No transformation is possible unless you truly dissect your inner and outer self. This has been the key to becoming a leader since the days of Socrates and Aristotle-"Know thyself." Leadership guru, Warren Bennis, states, "Know thyself means separating who you are and who you want to be from what the world thinks you are and wants you to be." An aboriginal proverb states that, **"A 1000 mile journey starts with a single step."** This single step is to know your self – your mental and physical characteristics. A good critical self-assessment brings in optimism, belief that your abilities are no way lacking and spots you need to look at and improve.

When you honestly evaluate which parts of your personality dynamics are assets and which ones are of concern, you have already moved beyond failure and cleared successfully the first step towards achieving success. Sometimes, how you deal with small day to day problems often denotes your attitudes to handling bigger problems in life. At times, there are certain hidden talents or major concerns and self-assessment helps in exploring these for larger benefits. From my personal experience of working in the industry and going through hundreds of annual appraisals, I rarely found employees self-assessing themselves honestly. Some leave the section blank, while others deliberately dodge the questions. This reflects their fear in being honest and truthful. They carry apprehensions that the organisation may make use of their self-assessment to their disadvantage. This fear keeps them away from the larger role it plays in their career development. Remember no one is born a great success achiever nor achieves success overnight. In order to be a competent success campaigner, you ought to know in detail about yourself and understand how you are going to drive yourself to accomplish your campaign.

Self-assessment is the process of looking at your self in order to assess aspects that are important to your individuality and helps identify key areas of achievements or failures. It involves ability to assess your own strengths and areas for improvements, formulating and pursuing your goals and unlearning and relearning new skills, attitudes and conduct. According to Lao Tzu, **"Knowing others is intelligence; knowing yourself is true wisdom. Mastering others is strength, mastering yourself is true power."** Research shows that by recognising and understanding your behavioural characteristics, you are likely to pursue the task in the right way and get suitable results. Beth Bledsoe, Director of Strategic Initiatives, Ingersoll Rand University opines that, **"If you want to be a great manager, there is a lot to learn. But the most fundamental lesson is that it starts with our own personal effectiveness. Know yourself. Listen to feedbacks. Build on your strengths. Do what you say you will do."** According to a news article, 'A Star is Made', published in the *New York Times*

Magazine((2006, May 7), 'Anders Ericsson, a researcher and professor of psychology at Florida State University refutes the commonly held notion that cognitive skills, particularly those like memory, are mostly genetically determined. He concluded that, the act of memorising is more a function of dedicated commitment and practice than a genetic gift. It involves setting specific goals, obtaining immediate feedbacks, and concentrating as much on technique as on the outcome.' **The report further suggests that often most people don't want to do a thing, not because they don't like it, but because they don't want to practise to perform better, they essentially lack the desire to excel**. It is recommended to carry a planned self- assessment on the following important parameters of your performance.

Make personal improvement plan

'Old habits die hard' and incorporating change initially meets with your mental blocks and resistance. So what will you do, plan meticulously improvements or keep shifting your planning. The choice is absolutely yours. Based on your own initial self-assessment and knowing yourself, what particular self- traits would you like to look at in-depth? What should you be doing to know yourself even better?

Self-observation

It is difficult to bring change in your overall self unless you have information on what you often do, think, feel and what your skills and capabilities are. This calls for determining when, why and under what conditions you currently use certain actions. For example, if you have underperformed in meeting a goal in the recent past, find out honestly why that happened. Believe me, we are most often aware of our shortcomings, but generally overlook these as a habit. Self-observation is a tool that helps dismantling the mental blocks for managing you to perform better. Just keep a mental record of observations on your actions and conduct even if you have committed mistake. This will encourage you to go back to the starting point to correct the mistake or change the direction of your action. It would be advisable to observe people known to you, who are successful or even someone whom you want to emulate, say your role model.

Personality traits

Personality essentially means the patterns of your thinking, conduct and behaving in a given situation. The personality build up is based on your inheritance genetically to a large extent and emotions, attitudes and motivation picked from your parents, family, culture, school and get added up with your interaction with the society as you grow in life. It essentially is your way of life, but can be improved and changed with practice. What are your inner and outer personality characteristics, such as thinking patterns, mind-set, feelings, emotions, values, actions and their suitable integration for success? How do you make choices/judgements? What are the personality related issues which trouble you off and on? Do you easily get stressed? Are you confronted with behavioural problems? Do you struggle with your energy levels? Are you temper and reaction-prone? Do you feel comfortable working in teams/individually?

Beliefs

What are the positive and negative opinions you hold about yourself. Are you capable of setting concise and specific goals and possess positive beliefs that you can achieve these? Do you steer yourself through crisis situations and have conviction about your beliefs that you can do it?

Experiences

Reflect on all the activities you have performed on your earlier attempts on success trail. Ask self questions, such as:

- ❑ What have you liked and disliked about each activity you performed?

- ❑ What did you learn from each activity?
- ❑ Which aspects of the task were problematic and need in-depth study and correction?

Self-confidence

How desperate is your zeal and keenness to achieve your success campaign? How strong is your enthusiasm to succeed? Do you take risks and be accountable. Are you unbendable enough to stay put in spite of hardships and obstacles? How good are you in managing fears? Are you adequately self-motivated to translate your passion to suitable action? Do you accept both positive and negative feedback and work on these accordingly and have realistic optimism levels? Do you believe in your self and have respect for your abilities, strengths and values?

Personal values

Do you believe in personal values, such as: cooperation, helping others, team spirit, service before self, transparency, integrity and honesty, reliability and self-discipline, etc? Values are beliefs you develop early in life and are shaped by your family, culture, education and different socialisation processes. Some values are maintained throughout your lives, while others may change.

Interpersonal skills

How good are your interpersonal skills? Do you look at your own personal behaviour or keep cribbing and criticising others for their poor behaviour. On your success campaign, you often need help and cooperation of others. You can avail their help provided you have good relationship skills. Are you aggressive or assertive in your dealings?

Skills Assessment

Skills are your abilities that are learnt through different activities including work, professional experiences and training. You can identify weaknesses in your skills and also become aware of those that you apply well. Some essential behavioural skills are: Communications, planning, discipline, introvert/extrovert, personality orientation, initiative, target achiever, decision making, commitment, convictions, etc. These are of course in addition to your job competencies/skills.

Weaknesses/ Concerns

Weaknesses are excess baggage which you have been carrying all these years without realising their adverse impact on you by creating mental blocks and building resistance to improvement. Most of your weaknesses are known to you and have become part of your habit and style. Often you may try to hide these from others and when brought to your notice, you may not accept, and instead give excuses. Most of your weaknesses are stationed in your subconscious mind and need to be worked on (For details, see chapter 12.) Focussing on your weaknesses is essential, but it is important to not get snowed under by just concentrating on gaps instead make plan for improvement step by step, attacking one weakness at a time and working wholeheartedly on it. Managing a weakness means taking possession of it, acknowledging it as part of you and not get disheartened. However, don't be so focussed on improving your weaknesses that you may neglect your strengths by default. Developing of new skills and improving the existing ones is important, but you should also spend time in knowing what you do well. Remember, each one of us has weakness, but the *success mantra is improving with constant practice.*

Strengths

Malcolm Forbes says that, **"Too many people overvalue what they are not and undervalue what they are."** Each one of you has strengths in terms of your inner and exterior personality dynamics. Can you identify these and develop trust in your abilities? The levels and percentages though vary among individuals. Look at the strengths as a self-consultant and recall whether you have been making full use of your strengths. Can you make value additions to these? Think about what makes you different than others. An excellent way to identify your strengths is to consider your achievements as these illustrate your abilities and skills and is indicative of your potential for taking initiative and solving problems. Your strengths should always be under your focus to keep you motivated to perform better.

Feedback

Most of you are reluctant to gather feedback because you are not only fearful of what others think of your performance, but also want to protect and enhance your self-image. Get out of this mental phobia and understand that opinions and views of others help you gain an insight into areas of your performance which need to be looked into depth for correction. Unless you interact, disclose your performance to others and work on the feedback, your self-assessment will be incomplete. You can accomplish this in an informal way by simply asking some trusted peers/boss, subordinates or friends to be honest and just offer some insight into how they perceive your performance. Feedback from different people can be a great source of highlighting your strengths and underlining skills that need to improve. This way you build a strong self-awareness and would be an asset on your success campaign. You can also observe how your peers/friends who are having a consistent success record or perform exceedingly well at work respond to and manage different situations. Compare the way you handle similar events and take corrective measures wherever required.

Past Achievements

Identify all the past achievements in your career, personal life and successes. This will help build awareness of your strengths and restore your confidence in your abilities, skills and renew your vigour.

Sample Evaluation

I have given here under few sample behavioural skills to give an idea for personal assessment. You may expand the list as per individual requirement and need.

1 Do you understand and use your feelings to relate to people well?

2 What are your prevailing personality traits and characteristics? No doubt, primary personality related characteristics don't change overnight, but with sustained efforts, practice and training, personality related characteristics can be changed to be your assets on the success campaign. So how do you plan to maximise these and what all you are prepared to sacrifice for it?

3 **Two important personal Beliefs to be changed/replaced:**

Belief 1 ______________________________

____

Action:

Belief 2______________________________

____

Action:

4. **Two important Feelings to be changed/replaced:**

Feeling 1 ______________________________

____

Action:

Feeling 2 ______________________________

____

5 **List out three inadequate key skills blocking your success.**

1. ____________ 2. ____________ 3. ____________

6. **List out specific time-bound actions to overcome these barriers to success.**

1. ____________ 2. ____________ 3. ____________

7. **List out three most important weaknesses in your inner personality dynamics:**

   1. ______________ 2. ______________ 3. ______________

8. **List out specific time-bound corrections:**

9. **Self-confidence building goals:**

Goal 1	Action	Goal 2	Action
Goal 3	Action	Goal 4	Action

10. **Persistency building goals:**

Goal 1	Action	Goal 2	Action

11. **Overall Self-assessment and feedback**

Blueprint for Success

Success is Moving Beyond Failure

In rebuilding your success campaign, there may be actions, often nervously stretched beyond your expectations and you have companions like emotions, feelings, uncertainties, failures, risks, fear, turns and twists and happy moments as well. It therefore **is a tight rope walk and like getting down the aisle in one piece fast and furious.** How to accomplish your mission therefore seems a million dollar question and may have numerous responses and expressions depending on your goal? Your objectives of attaining success may vary, such as making more money, acquiring a challenging job, academic pursuits, relationship, health, etc. No doubt choosing to be successful is an obvious and unchallenged wish every one possesses. But does it happen overnight without working for it? No never! Success is commitment, wholehearted dedication, having a definite goal and a strategy for its attainment. Just imagine- why shouldn't you earn reasonably well to discharge your responsibilities and have a good night sleep? Why can't you feel motivated and passionate each morning about your purpose, work and responsibilities? Of course, success to you would be a failure if you don't believe in values, self-development and incorporate personal transformation in terms of proactive behaviour and positive attitudes. **Success is not only having tons of money, power, high status, job and assets; it is accepting failure and working on it.** Success doesn't mean avoiding risks and walking on the sideways of rejection and failure. It is initiative, self-driven habit and leading from the front. It is looking for new avenues of growth, developing an analytical mind-set and taking decisions. It is not being dejected every now and then, going home at night and complaining. It is living patiently with struggles, committing mistakes, rectifying these and moving beyond failures. It is a lifetime campaign and a neverending process, where each time success is achieved, it becomes a pedestal for next, and the process continues till your last breath. In pursuit of success, there are neither intervals nor shelters to take rest on your journey. It is a continued struggle till you are able to cross the winning line.

Before moving ahead on your success campaign, it is absolutely essential to understand the larger picture of what success is, and what is that you are looking for and what in turn, you are prepared to do. No doubt, there may be occasions when inspiration and enthusiasm depletes on facing failure and makes your perseverance complicated and doubtful. This is the crucial phase of your success campaign and decides the future course of action. However, in practice, some of you may become fearful, pessimist and naysayer, and reflect your character by giving depressing answers while undertaking a goal- "I tried. It is not working." "I am too tired." "Can I look at it on Monday etc?" Surprisingly, replies such as these that one commonly hears are just tattered, ragged and sooner put you out of reckoning. **Success is sacrificing extra leisure, time off and material comfort. It is do it now or never and go beyond the imaginary boundaries of your limitations.** It is putting in extra horsepower and sticking through good times, sad times and changing times and above all, remain hovering with a relentless mind. You need to learn from disciplined animals like dogs, bulls and horses who exemplify through their courage, endurance, discipline, persistency and guts. Success after a long-drawn-out battle with struggles and resistance ultimately becomes like a **bottle full of honey.., you keep on thumping the bottom hard, and little later honey starts oozing all at once making you believe that, 'nothing wins like winning.'** This is a time when you feel at ease with yourself because you are accomplishing your campaign and building on your self-esteem, creating positive influence and aura around.

Just imagine if your success was without hiccups and glitches? Wouldn't success be devoid of flavour, colour, revelations and being an eye-opener? It is only when you make obstructions and hindrances your torchbearer that you realise – "My God what all I went through." The feelings are euphoric and joys similar to what you feel when you happen to climb successfully to the top of a rocky and rugged mountain. You can't stop tweeting to self – **"I am in the seventh heaven."** The excitement is boundless, elation limitless and stimulus par excellence. A pat on the flipside is- 'A job well done'. For example, you need to learn from thousands of students from India and other countries who go to West for advanced studies every year without any parental help, yet they make success spot for themselves. They slog with part time meager work by washing dishes or swiping floor, sharing rooms with many, yet keep up with their studies and academic projects. They never shed tears nor make their parents back home cry because of their menial part time work and undergoing other hardships of cross-cultural barriers. **As devotion and desperation are vital to success, so is the passion of climbing the mountain of failures with a great deal of preparation and planning.**

We are all born with power of inner drive to create our own situations. Some are able to convert these to their advantage in the first go and become successful, while some take time and go through the failure route before finding the hidden treasures of success. Achieving success calls for obsession, a bull-headed approach to make a head start and a habit and psyche of a hungry loin. Over and over again, you may hear about people who are underdogs and suddenly emerge from nowhere and stand tall on a success splash seemingly possessing supernatural powers. Some of them may have the lady luck, but majority are focussed on making a mark for themselves. They are well aware that craving to see the sight of their dream may shatter if they get bogged down by distress, setbacks and failures? With a strong longing for success at their backs, they build stamina to go up the ladder by sticking to a game plan and carrying it through.

Success Mantra

We all like dreaming and making castles in the air, but achieving dreams happens only when you are conscious and awaken. Success is dreaming, visualising and learning that being in the moment as the experience soars throughout the body and mind is the secret to effective artistry. In essence, there is no single path to success and neither is it determined by your exterior postures, clothes, beauty/ handsomeness or the fancy tags some carry. Not even by driving spunky cars, staying in sea view apartments or drinking the most expensive liquor. **Success essentially is a 'do-it-yourself project'. You are the story writer, director, producer and actor of your dream movie. Like each hour each day, you shape the dialogues, perform acts, make changes, enact songs and dance, etc. As you build the film scene by scene with absolute synchronisation day by day, so you do by stitching together hard work, struggles, hardships and taking risks at every stage to build on your success.** It is binding yourself to a pledge, fortitude, consistency and keeping up with the vigour to fight till the task is accomplished. The success mantra is best explained by the following brief fascinating stories:

- *While visiting America, a man went into a cafeteria in lower Manhattan to eat. He sat down at an empty table and waited for someone to take his order. Of course, nobody did. Finally, a woman with a tray full of food sat down opposite him and informed him how a cafeteria worked. "Start out at that end," she said. "Just go along the line and pick out what you want. At the other end, they'll tell you how much you have to pay." "I soon learnt that's how everything works in America," the person told a friend. "Life's a cafeteria here. You can get anything you want as long as you are willing to pay the price.* ***You can***

***even get success, but you'll never get it if you wait for someone to bring it to you. You have to get up and get it yourself.*"** (Excerpts:inspirationalstories.com)

- *Abraham Lincoln always carried on his person some newspaper clippings that adorned his achievements. The most significant being a letter written by the reformer, John Bright to an American newspaper editor, speaking highly of Lincoln's leadership and his success in the re-election as President in the former year. Lincoln used this as a tool of inner strength when things were looking lackluster or when despair settled over his mind and he could reach into his pocket and find hope.*
- *The movie "Point Break", released in 1991 starring Keanu Reeves and Patrick Swayze, is yet another fine example of success mantra. Reeves starts as a footballer but hurts his knee and decides to train for being an FBI agent. Throughout the movie, he displays his winning attitude by hunting down a group of bank robbers. In the end, he decides that being an FBI agent isn't the right thing for him because he has to compromise his most important principles: honesty, loyalty and integrity. Swayze also has a winning attitude and chooses to become the best surfer but gets into robbing banks to make fast buck. It takes Reeves' best effort and persistence to catch Swayze. Reeves turn to be successful, while Swayze was destined to fail because of a deficit in his objective. In the end, Swayze is forced to choose a tragic death.*

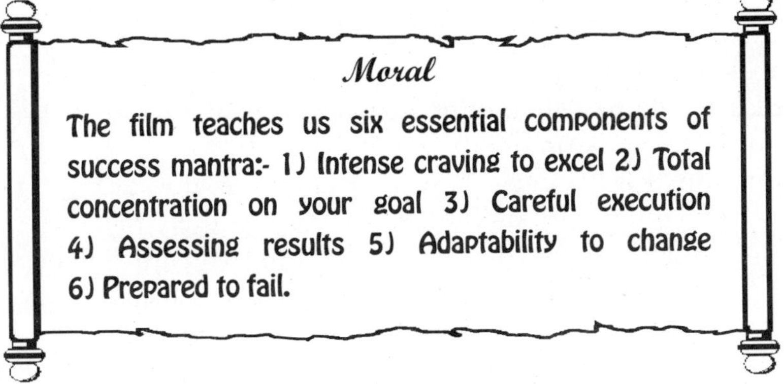

Moral

The film teaches us six essential components of success mantra:- 1) Intense craving to excel 2) Total concentration on your goal 3) Careful execution 4) Assessing results 5) Adaptability to change 6) Prepared to fail.

As said earlier, success is a brand that generates fascination and a strong emotional connect with your inner world that results in producing drive of the highest order which becomes your infatuation and ardour. What then is the *mantra* of achieving a well-deserved success? Warren Buffett, world's third richest man believes that its passion about your work. **"Enjoy your work and do it with passion. All the good things will follow."** He says that, "I totally trust the people who run their businesses. I started on a blank canvas with an idea on how I wanted my corporation to be. All I tell entrepreneurs whom I work with is 'here's another brush. Create your own painting'." Oprah Winfrey says that, "The big secret in life is that there is no big secret. Whatever your goal, you can get there if you're willing to work."

Making a Goal without a Goalkeeper is no Success

Making a goal without a goalkeeper is nothing but success devoid of elegance and thrill. If there was no one guarding the goal post, there would be no real kick in making a goal. What I am trying to emphasise is that true success means crossing over failures and adversities to make a real excitement out of it. It's not like taking over the legacy of family business and not performing to take it beyond where it was left by your forefathers. Not everyone can become JRD Tata, GD Birla or Dhirubhai Ambani. They were destined to bring laurels to Indian business and industry and put it on the international map. They were firm believers that there was no solitary path to success, but a whole lot of failure-alluring habits that ultimately lead them to astounding success. While on one hand, each success brings in better emoluments, increased responsibilities, authority and accountability and on the other hand, it slowly makes you loner and losing day to day touch with team members. This is when fears to maintain success and prestige creeps in. Therefore, while planning next move up the ladder; do change the priorities but make it a point to keep in touch with people. **To me the success equation is somewhat like:**

Success = Manure (mind energy/positive attitudes/ failure) + **Sunlight** (/goal / luck/opportunity) + **Water** (Hard work/persistency/ desperation/) = **Achievement.**

Enriching Success

A story goes that, "A very strong woodcutter asked for a job in a timber merchant's firm, and he got it. The pay was really good and so were the work conditions. For that reason, the woodcutter was determined to do his best. His boss gave him an axe and showed him the area where he was supposed to work. The first day, the woodcutter brought 18 trees "Congratulations," the boss said. "Go on that way!" Very motivated for the boss' words, the woodcutter tried harder the next day, but he only could bring 15 trees. The third day he tried even harder, but he only could bring 10 trees. Day after day, he was bringing less and less trees. "I must be losing my strength," the woodcutter thought. He went to the boss and apologised, saying that he could not understand what was going on. **"When was the last time you sharpened your axe?" the boss asked. "Sharpen? I had no time to sharpen my axe. I have been very busy trying to cut trees..."** (Ref: Stephen Covey, 7 Habits of Highly Effective People).

Moral of the Story: An appraisal of the previous achievements helps to tighten belts in the weak areas so that next in line is excellence in success. With each success, there is need to sharpen your focus and mental skills.

Successful are always found making tough resolutions that are out of reach of the common people. They always focus on finding solution to the obstacle, while a failure sees every obstacle as a problem and excuse not to perform. What made the great Frank Sinatra set the standard for pop phrasing? What makes the great Indian melody queens Lata Mangeshkar and Asha Bhonsle still going great guns? Simple, great performers act upon from their soul with passion and emotions to invoke the holy blessings. As said earlier, success is neither bound by age nor by race, one is unaware when your intellect gets activated backed by some luck and some opportunity. Take a look:

It was amazing to know how a 6-year old Leo Hunter, Potter book fan from UK has challenged the famous, such as J.K. Rowling, Cheryl Cole in writing stories. During August 2010, he penned a small novel about his pet dog 'Me and My Best Friend' which has bagged a multi-book publishing deal from Strategic Book Publishing in the US.A. It is a real feat indeed. Only some time back, his teacher in school had said that Leo needed to improve on his story writing skills. The school was amazed so were others on his excellence in story writing and an overnight international celebrity status at such a young age.

The key to success will always remain:

Persistent…Passion…Perspiration…Perfection… Penchant Patience…Positive…Practice…Prayer…

No one has domination on success, neither you, nor me. On accomplishing success, do not become egotistical or conceited. You are still an ordinary human being, the same as the next fellow in spite of your acquired money or power. Be humble, friendly and helpful to others. I feel achieving success is not as difficult as maintaining and stabilising it. While success brings in triumph, power, elation, respect, etc. but it also brings in whole lot of responsibilities, discipline, increased maturity and greater emphasis on personal behaviour. Successful need to be mentally prepared to **'laugh and the world laughs with them, weep and they weep alone.'** As said in the earlier chapters, care needs to be taken that in the urge for more and more, you don't lose track of success and instead land on the path to failure. Power often is the manifestation of success and assuming power can sometimes lead to a personal disaster. One can be a big star, a legend and a role model to millions, yet a small mistake can lead to a massive failure.

"Most people spend their lives building financial houses of straws, which are susceptible to wind, fire, rain and big bad wolves."

– Robert T Kiyosaki

The late GD Birla, famous industrialist was once asked the secret of his success in building one of the largest business empires in India. He said, "What you call success is judged by others as failure." Success is often like walking on the sharp edge of a sword. **Meteoric rise often has meteoric fall.** Decision making may at times become waterloo of successful because often success blurrs decision making more because of getting carried away under the intoxication of power. Success, no doubt is a dream come true, but it may soon turn to a severe nightmare and lead to a personal disaster if the mind power is directed to enjoying the illegitimate perks of the position, fame and extra constitutional authority. I feel if success goes to head which does happen to some, it ultimately leads to a major failure. Take for example, the case of Rupert Murdoch, an Australian American media mogul and the Chairman and CEO of News Corporation. The News International phone hacking scandal by the erstwhile News of the World publication in the UK belonging to Murdoch in 2011 has created ripples and history on invading the privacy of individuals by phone taping. The all powerful Murdoch was grilled by British Parliament for his inadequate corporate governance for which he was brought to his knees and he profoundly apologised. **Success is command and authority that is like a magnet from which it is difficult to keep away and distracted for long.** It often leads to feathering your own nests. Remember power has wings like the giant dinosaurs and it takes no time to fly off and get demagnetised and marginalised. Therefore **respect, adore and be humble with the use of power if success has to continue unabated**.

Garnering Success

- Jack Welch of GE fame once said, "Winning is about having the best people in your team. It doesn't help if you're surrounded by people who are less talented than you are." Past research shows that high performing organizations ensure that their human resource has: shared understanding, well-defined objectives, clear individual goals, competencies and knowledge, requisite skills, sharing of commitments etc.

- Being happy is a sign of stable emotions, thoughts, and focus that normally leads to success. Both happiness and accomplishment are related to the state of mind. Winners understand that their thoughts, attitudes and habits are the foundation of their beliefs. They become self-change agents to incorporate desired improvements. They don't have a mysterious wand to change their lives. They work hard on their behaviour-related weaknesses before they start working for success. It would be extremely useful to draw inspirations from the legendary Carl Lewis, who once said that, ***"I may be walking slowly but I never walk backwards and whenever; I walk backwards it's only for a long jump."***
- Success achievers possess a winning attitude which is like a self-doctrine and an ideology to aspire to headway often right from their childhood. They b*uild a strong foundation of trust, self-assurance, and spotlight and continuously work on creating a conflictless mind.*
- Comprehending the importance of transforming thinking, feelings and beliefs. If you constantly think and look positive, your mind will do the rest.
- The mental images making rounds of your mind are the key factors behind your thinking and action. Use the imagination to picture images of what you want to achieve and mentally rotate this picture through mind, heart, and other vitals of the body so that every important body function is in rhythm and synchronises with your imagination. Visualising positive aspects of life sooner or later change to realities.
- Sometimes dreaming miracles happening to you and seeing yourselves riding the rugby horse to success develops the inner urge to perform. Imagine you are

sitting in a race course and mentally whipping the champion horse of success.

One needs to learn from the trout fish species that swims upstream in search of cold water, its habitat. Success is not just a bowl of candies alone; but citation as well. The real successful cherish a life that they make by pursuing higher goals and keeping their feet entrenched on the ground. They live for today and in this moment, plan and work for tomorrow. They 'make hay while the sun shines' because they are well aware that success and failure can change hands any moment.

Major Tips for Attaining Success

1. When there is a failure and success appears farfetched, you should preferably go in for diet control and start jogging/brisk walk/exercises, etc. I feel controlling on diet and performing daily jog is most difficult to follow rigorously and needs a high order of persistency. **If you are unrelenting to make small strides each day, you surely build a base for self- motivation, re-knock and revive your enthusiasm to get back to trudging.**
2. Gaining height and distance doesn't come without exertion and sweating. Can you therefore be **prepared to stick out your neck, get off your bump and make things happen to carry success home and fulfill your dreams.**
3. No one knows how and when success strikes. When that happens, be prepared to grab it, do justice with it so that it remains and does not fly away. **Success is raring to go and habituated with no waiting because it shifts and jumps from one person to another within no time.**
4. Success comes at a cost in terms of being on pins and needles and there is no tomorrow. Start working on the goal right there and then. **Success is through and through keenness on way to your clear and concise intention.**

5. Brand success dazzles and stands out if it is built step by step in spite of scanty resources, being repeatedly unlucky and without assets to fall back upon.
6. Accomplishments in life are an outcome of tolerance, firmness, decisiveness, cultivating the right habits and of course, a bit of luck. **Success likes to be with those who not only dream to achieve the highest but grind for it and do not compromise for average returns. Once they achieve success, their next target is excellence in success.**
7. Success is not a commodity that can be purchased in the market place. It is not available as a charity or gratis nor is every second person successful. **Success belongs to you if you are prepared to be unsuccessful, become desperate, get worn out by working hard and keep awake nights together. It belongs to you if you have a clear road map to your destination.**
8. Do not show off self by packaging exterior looks, body language, conversing like a parrot. Success is not making eloquent boardroom presentations or performing drawing room conversations as is prevalent sometimes in the corporate world. Instead back the success campaign by super performance, confidence, self-belief, trust, personal values, being humble and above all par excellence in professiona skills.
9. Never ever feel that accomplishments belong onl to heavy investors in stock markets/industrialists executives in boardrooms, great athletes and sportspersons, media barons and film stars, etc. **I also belongs to those who sprout as an ordinary person; take the brunt of tornado like situations in their resolve to move beyond failures. Success is 'he who laughs last, laughs the longest.'**
10. Accomplishing the success campaign is a long-drawn battle **and needs servicing regularly and discarding complacency, sluggishness and slowness.** Constan

endeavour and endurance is what will eventually swim you across. **Spin or drop, move ahead or get left behind, the choice remains with you and your doggedness.**

11. Like the failure, all successful too have limitations and weaknesses. The difference is that successful try hard to impair their shortcomings, but the unsuccessful often repent and live with their shortcomings, deficiency, limitations and narrow vision.

I feel if money and physical assets alone were a measure of success, then many gamblers, black marketeers, hoarders, bootleggers, smugglers, power brokers and underworld mafias would score the highest on success quotient. Having financial security is undoubtedly a psychological boost, but what about those who are not lucky enough to have this, yet they survive and have success goals to achieve.

Boost up Your Mind Power

> *"Mind O Mind magic and mystery;*
> *for it dates back to history.*
> *Mind O Mind rewinds the past,*
> *for it runs in the future so fast.*
> *Mind' O Mind is attention and retention,*
> *for it actually is a divine intervention.*
> *Mind O Mind is action and reaction*
> *for its creation and destruction."*
>
> *–Barkha Dhar*

Having understood the real manifestations of success and what it calls for, you next need to understand what human mind power is and how it helps you to achieve your objectives and goals in life. Mind is the sum total of your thoughts and observations and is blessed with unlimited potential and power. It is more than a think machine that powers you through wisdom, creativity, feelings, judgement, destruction and evil. The choice to direct mind's energy and endurance however is absolutely with you.

Take a look at the following story:-

> *A jungle was inhabited by scores of monkeys. One day a cap seller on way to the village felt tired and took rest under a tree in the jungle. After some time, he heard whooping sounds of monkeys and the moment he looked around, to his utter surprise, he saw the bag full of caps*

was empty and all the caps were taken away by the monkeys and put on their respective heads. The cap seller became angry and threw stones at the monkeys sitting on the tree. The monkeys in turn plucked fruits and threw at the cap seller. This went on for some time. The cap seller sat down thinking what he should do to retrieve the caps from the monkeys. Taking a clue from the habit of throwing fruits at the cap seller and application of mind, he suddenly removed the cap from his head and threw it on the ground. The monkeys have a habit of copying. Each copied and threw caps at the ground. The cap seller collected the caps and continued happily his journey.

Moral

Your mind can put you either in troubles and hardships or steer you away to success. It entirely depends on the proper application of mind.

The most important part of our planet has been the evolution of human mind which is so complex, unique, mysterious and yet an unparallel creation. In spite of hundreds of experiments, extensive research, hundreds of books and treatise written, extensive debates carried the world over, yet mind remains a mystery. It is blessed with unlimited potential and power. It is like a magnet that attracts everything concerning our life because we are surrounded by energy. Our environment, ecology, solar system and every other thing around us is just the manifestation of energy in its basic form. The brighter side of human mind has been that of creating wonders. From rubbing stones to producing fire, from Newton's laws of motion to Einstein's theory of relativity, from finding water droplets on moon to the internet, from Shakespeare's 'Romeo and Juliet' to

Wordsworth's, 'A thing of beauty is a joy forever', from Picasso's dreams on canvas to M F Hussain's painting on Indian women, from controlling cancer cells to attempting create an artificial brain are just few creations of human side of this mysterious mind.

Discussing briefly the subject of mind in this book seems of much significance as **your mind is a preface to your success and failure**. Like a czar, it governs your cognitive and emotive abilities, connects you to people and surroundings and brings in life's essential lessons through good and bad experiences. Most of you would understand what I am trying to highlight is to tame and control your mind. This certainly is a difficult task, but not impossible. To start such taming, you need to generate positive vibes through periodical scanning of your thoughts and thinking patterns. Such change goes miles in getting rid of the superfluous in life and slowly enables to mount up on the saddle of your mind horse just to direct yourself of a sapient route. To make things happen, you first have to turn on your mind power, lay your hands on the control button and unleash and enter your peak state. Rightly said by Franklin D. Roosevelt that, **"Men and women are not prisoners of fate, but only prisoners of their own minds."** Amazingly most people tap the energy from mind into its full capacity where success is defined as **'20 percent physical and 80 percent mental'.** In fact, it is stated that on an average, we only use 10% of our mind's full power, leaving 90% unused. American psychologist William James once said, "Compared to what we should be, we are only half alive. We are making use of only a small part of our mind power. Deep down inside of us are vast powers we know nothing of and never use."

Generally, people are unaware that their mind is made up of two powerful sections, i.e., **conscious and subconscious** that often does not work in synchronisation. The conscious part is active when you are awake and always tries to boss around and have its way. It thinks, reasons, plans and directs all actions of the body, determines results, makes decisions and takes logical and analytical path based on reasoning. It registers pain and pleasure and even sets your goals. The conscious mind makes choices, almost every minute of your lives. The sub-conscious mind on the other hand is an auto-pilot in your brain that is dormant 24x7 and is like a serene ocean that is most of the time quiet and typical. The subconscious mind is neither logical nor rational and doesn't judge whether things are working or not and develops programmes that operate automatically. It operates deep beneath your consciousness and stores what you see, hear, touch and smell.

If you look at life profoundly, starting from the day a child is born; you will observe that his senses are activated the moment he is born but the child's mind is like a blank sheet of paper. It is only when the child grows up, say three years onwards; the parents assume the role of an artist and start drawing pictures and images of a particular personality and behaviour through their own thoughts and actions. However, children vary widely in their skills of application of mind. It is the mother who is the first Guru and plays a predominant role in developing abilities. Early experience and interaction with the environment are most critical in a child's brain development. From such initial explanation of lifespan development, we can say that our mind seems like a combination of our past *karma* and also of similarity of the picture drawn on our blank mind by our parents and the things we do and experience as we grow in life and encounter challenges. While our parents may have made up our mind to what it may be today, but we have the power to change it to what we feel and experience that is best for us.

You can be your own artist by studying your mind and the changes you want to incorporate. In addition, your past experiences, feelings and beliefs leave deep impressions. The moment you start gradually changing impressions one by one, it leads to change in your thinking and actions. For example, if your goal is to obtain 90 % marks in the examination and you end getting just 80% marks, you haven't failed because you are in the process of trying and haven't stopped. If you give up thinking that this is something that's impossible, then at that very moment you have failed. This elucidates **that failures do not happen**

until you choose them by a certain way of thinking or doing. For instance: When you get angry, feel jealous or hate someone, you may wish bad for him. While on other occasions, when you are positive and happy, your mind generates feelings, such as loving and helping others, etc. These positive and negative thoughts are generated in your subconscious mind and represent a sum total of your past experiences and beliefs. Part of such mental activity is primarily due to the conditioning of your minds by your parents early on in your life like blindfolding the eyes of a horse and part of it is due to your strong likes and dislikes which you may pick up as you go on in life. This is how knowingly or unknowingly you build values, beliefs and perceptions that either encourage or discourage you to change. In order to move beyond failure and graduate to success, you first need to work on your mind:

- Carry a total audit of your thoughts, actions, observations, attitudes and behaviour stage by stage.
- Try to de-programme your mind from fear and gradually, replace it with confidence and determination to succeed with repeated attempts.

To tap it:

- Your thoughts, beliefs and feelings are the core habitants of your subconscious, and unsettling these habitants is a difficult task, and at the same time necessary too. Great achievers work on their subconscious before launching an onslaught on success.
- Nobody is able to live a smooth life uninterrupted. People tend to have bumps in life, which reduces a fast pace to a slow expedition. Navigating journey however is entirely your decision. For instance, only few self-assess and make attempts at conditioning their minds and the vibes it produces. Majority instead hold a doctorate in analysing and criticising thinking and actions of others- **'I am right, he is not'**...... You must remember that changing even few characteristics of your behaviour is a long drawn affair

that requires working with a strong commitment. It is like learning how to spell or use grammar or even practise arithmetic doing it over and over again.

Success is a mind game

Success, undoubtedly is a game of mind, your self-fulfilment and self-prophecy that **'nothing sells like success'** which leaves a permanent happy mark on your lives. The sooner you pick up the threads, the better off and advantageous you become. Never mind if in spite of a samurai ambush, yet you fail to make it. At least, you gave a nail-biting challenge, had an incredible feeling and got through heap of sensations. The secret to success is painful and demanding practice and hard work. For example, amateur singers take a singing lesson; they experience it as fun, a release of tension. But professional singers, it's the opposite: They increase their concentration and focus on improving their performance during the lesson. Success means training mind to the ups and downs in life and stabilising feelings to face hardships. Developing a mind-set for garnering success requires becoming a self-change agent to incorporate desired improvements by working hard on your behaviour related weaknesses. *Building a strong foundation of trust, self-assurance and focus, and continuously working on creating a conflictless mind.*

Guidelines to Drive Mind Power

1. Check feelings

The first time kids go to play with a group of children; their experience is not memorable since for the first time, they are left alone with strangers. Some smart ones bully them and make them cry, while others look at them and make fun, few start to play with them. By the time they understand and became receptive to their surroundings, happiness, excitement, fear, insecurity and a host of other feelings have already risen in the subconscious. Similarly, whenever you are in an unfamiliar situation like the first day in college or a job, etc., you feel stressed, fearful and out of place and your subconscious mind immediately flashes childhood memories of your first experiences in interacting with others in life. Altering feelings to accommodating ones by identifying the source and releasing the built up thoughts by practice gradually brings in new hope and a behavioural change helping in your success campaign. Often you may be wondering why some people seem to have everything in their lives, while others struggle on a day to day basis? This is because some people have feelings that are pre-programmed into the mind and that may be sabotaging their attempts to accomplishments. Luck, of course, has some role to play.

Feeling of underperformance or fear of failure arises basically from a negative belief about yourself and possibly due to a past failure. As already mentioned, the subconscious mind has both positive and negative feelings churned out of your beliefs, sentiments and life experiences. To mutate such negativity into positives, write downbeat feelings on a paper and against each question its authenticity. If you modify your perception about your sentiments, there are more chances of getting over the unhelpful feelings sooner than later. Similarly, alter negative self-talk which goes on in your mind to positive and optimistic. Keep assessing negative feelings one by one and think whether these have helped to grow or retracted you from achieving your success campaign? Repeatedly practising such amends slowly helps to overcome shallow feelings. For example, some of you may be afraid of swimming for fear of drowning. Feelings of fear stop you from learning. Likewise some people are afraid of crossing a busy road if they had an accident in the past. Past reminisces of a tragic incident leaves strong feelings in your mind that sometimes hinders you from even crossing a busy road alone. How you feel about something will always determine or affect what you do and how well you do it and the resultant outcome. So the next thing you need to do is to evaluate feelings going inside your mind and try to find how these have been responsible for any wrong moves in your life. If there has been a recent failure, find out what role feelings played and work on these for corrections.

2. Use of affirmations, "Yes, I Can"

Most of you are in the habit of starting with negative perceptions about situations, people and events in your lives. Sometimes unconsciously you repeat negative and pessimistic statements without realising their harmful affect on you. For example, "It is difficult. I know I will fail." "My manager is biased and would never consider me for promotion." These or similar thoughts result in making your subconscious mind stagnant. Affirmations are positive and constructive strokes that open up your mind to possibilities of altering your views on things and situations that appeared previously out of your understanding. With the use of affirmations, you are able to gradually delete the earlier junk feelings and beliefs and replace these with the new 'constructive and optimistic affirmations.' Positive Affirmations are like *success mantras* that need to be regularly chanted. While saying to yourself, **"I can do it" or 'I will do it',** you hone your mind's untapped talent and feed it with optimism. For instance, your child is not good at Mathematics and gets low grades. You try to provide support by way of coaching. If there are no improvements, you may start saying "you fool, you can't do it." But if you boost his confidence, take it up as a challenge and repeatedly tell him, "you can do it," your child will send positive signals to his subconscious mind and attune himself to a positive affirmation. What is being suggested is a **thorough brainwashing of your downbeat feelings**. For instance:

Unhelpful Thought	Helpful Thought
I am not worth anything.	I am a valuable person.
I have never accomplished anything.	I have accomplished many things.
I am poor at work.	I do many things well.

Daily reciting mentally optimistic affirmations are an important component of self-development and unlearning and relearning. For instance:

- ❑ I am highly impatient. It affects my interpersonal relationships and listening…to…. I need to improve upon my tolerance levels.
- ❑ Often people tell me that I overreact. Even my children feel the same way…to... I need to control my behavioural reactions and think twice before speaking.

For example, you want to learn driving, but all along have had a phobia that it is difficult and cannot be learnt. Every time you initiated learning, you left it half way because you felt you will meet up with an accident. The moment you became convinced and determined that you have to learn driving, you send vibes of conviction and confidence to your subconscious mind to act. With focus on learning and chanting *mantra* of you can drive the car, you will notice a change in your outlook and motivation. **The key to success therefore lies in the commands you give to the subconscious mind for amend**. There may be odd delays in achieving your success campaign, but that should not dishearten you, instead increase your resolve.

3. Proactive behaviour

Behaviour is the backbone of your success or failure and comprises basically of your thinking, actions and attitudes about a certain task/ situation. Actions based on your thinking decide whether you will be successful or meet a failure. These are also based on your choices and influence of circumstances. No doubt if your actions are right, these generally produce right results. Of course, there are other factors, such as goal setting, focus, implementation, style, hard work and your desperation levels to perform which are equally important.

4. Changing beliefs

There are no limits to what your subconscious mind will do for you through your belief system. If you have a notion that it's unlikely for you to be a CEO, your subconscious will do everything in its power to see that your belief comes true. The subconscious mind does not discriminate when it comes to thoughts, feelings and beliefs; it responds to fearful as well as peaceful thoughts. As said earlier, most of your beliefs are of childhood creation and as you go on in life, additions and alterations take place. At times, I feel belief is like carving on a stone that is hard to erase. Some times, even if you are told that your belief is wrong and misrepresents your personality, yet there are chances that you would hardly budge away from it because you have grown up putting with it since childhood. Also possibly these beliefs may have helped you temporarily in your past success campaigns. A closer look at your beliefs calls for a deeper understanding of your mind before attempting to change your beliefs. Some of these postulations are difficult to change as these appear to be deep-rooted in your mind. I have always believed that **changing behavioural dynamics might appear difficult and cumbersome, but it isn't impossible**. Changing beliefs is like treating an ailment or affliction that requires patience, courage and determination to cope.

The best way to change the past belief is by listing your ideas about work, relationships, people and situations in general. Against each, write whether these have been useful or created problems in your growth. Highlight the ones which limit growth and need changing. Against these limiting beliefs, write positive convictions after thinking and also observing attitudes of people who are successful. For example, you want to go for a morning jog and for this, you have to get up at 5 AM but most of the time, you are unable to make it because you get up late. Write down the beliefs which are creating hindrance to get up at 5 in the morning and go for a jog. For example, you can write "because I sleep late and therefore, I can't get up early or I watch late night movies on TV or I freak out regularly and come back home late, etc." By writing same or similar thoughts that influence your not getting up at 5 AM and going for a jog is the best way to uncover your beliefs and have a hard look at these. Often when you bring out beliefs from a hidden cave in your mind, it helps you to plan and implement corrective measures. Several times in a day repeat the positive enabling beliefs and use these at work. This is how gradually you will transform your old beliefs to new and positive ones. For example: in a study conducted by scientists, 'some people were given coffee to go to bed and the others were given milk. The next morning the people who drank coffee complained of a bad night's sleep. And the people who drank milk said they had a good night's sleep. Unknown to the participants, the caffeine had been removed from the coffee and added to the milk! 'The subjects believed that caffeine would keep them awake and the milk would help them sleep.'

5. Changing Mind Programming

The main architects of your mind programming are your parents, teachers and friends in school/college. When you grow as adults often what the mind thinks to be true becomes true. No matter what all you do, if you do not have a proper and dynamic mind programming that supports and helps achieve your goal, you will not thrive. For example, if you want to succeed and your mind programming is set on feeling that the goal is difficult to achieve and that you are not sure for success, no matter how hard you work, you will unconsciously draw failure instead of success. Putting many productive hours of work will only be useful if you change and eliminate what is not serving your desire and replace it with what you desire. Believe in the power of your subconscious mind because one of the most powerful ways to program your subconscious mind is through your belief systems. What the thinker (conscious mind) thinks, the prover (subconscious mind) proves. Beliefs are taken as instructions to the subconscious mind.

The following steps will be always useful:

1. First decide on what is your goal. Be specific and concise. No general ideas will work. Your subconscious mind then gets activated and will come up with ideas to make it happen.

2. Ensure your goal is realistic. For example, becoming a senior manager from junior manager may not happen overnight. Therefore, break your goals to meaningful achievements. Think in ways that will not set up a conflict between your thoughts and your feelings. For example, if you want to address a largely attended conference, visualise yourself addressing a large gathering and participants giving you a rousing ovation. Prof. Erantha De Mel in his latest book – 'Optimising the Infinite Mind' states that, "If you try to understand the mind processes and resolve to change your mind, you can change your life."
3. Display positive quotes, motivational messages both at home and at work and also read some good motivational self-help books as well as watch training videos. Your spouse, siblings, parents or friends can act as referees to remind you should you deviate from what is displayed through posters. Couple of reminders and comments of not obeying what is displayed will do the trick in due course of time. Habits die hard but repeated observations and taunts help in making change.

Summing up

Napoleon Hill once said that, **"Whatever the mind can conceive and believe it can achieve."** Taking a parallel from this, understand that the passport to a successful personal change happens only through a distinct journey inside your mind. This is to know about your self, where you stand today, your limitations and how you can drive power of your subconscious to meet your desires. No change is possible unless you are prepared to remove mental blocks, learn, experiment and wipe out the unwanted.

Developing a Positive and Agile Mind-set

By now you would have appreciated that a positive, upbeat and optimistic mind-set is the power behind your personal effectiveness and self-management. The important role the subconscious mind plays in your mental makeup is in essence your brand ambassador. Mind-set comprises essentially of attitudes, thoughts, feelings and conduct. It is a self-driven process and begins by getting rid of fears, past disappointments, letdowns and firming up belief in the self. It is said that 'winners do things differently'. I say **'winners outclass through their winning mind-set'.** Based on their strong belief system that is well woven in their psyche, they are able to direct their mental power to the winning temper in spite of hurdles, obstacles, letdowns and failures. It is common to witness how some individuals conquer each challenge by shear upbeat feelings, positive outlook and flexibility in approach. Even in case of underperformance, they remain calm, focussed and hopeful and manage it by creating an aura of encouraging feelings and good temperament around. Due to their constructive, helpful attitudes and habits, people are eager to emulate them as their role model.

There is a reasoned theme, direction and great message in the famous saying, ***'You can't direct the wind, but you can adjust your sails.'*** What is being advised is that even if there is a letdown, yet you can be in total command of yourself and project an upbeat image provided you change direction and course of your action and reaction? Your mind-set often reflects unconsciously life perspectives and your response to these. Developing and sustaining an optimistic state of mind really starts from you by believing in self, building an atmosphere of cheerful feelings around and seeing others in an affirmative way. This is possible by self- introspection and repeated practice. Most people often overlook and neglect developing positive expressions and thus, end up becoming their own worst enemy. ***A constructive and hopeful mind-set is indispensable and essential prerequisite for accomplishing your success campaign.***

History vouches and salutes truly successful people for having developed a habit of winning mind-set and being in charge of their careers by fuelling the force within them that set them apart from thousands. Their positive mind-set gave them energy that stimulated them to reach their true potential and established themselves as icons. Some well known examples to emulate are that of: Lee Iacocca former CEO, Chrysler Corporation and President, Ford Motors, Bill Clinton, Bill Gates. Indra Nooyi, the Chairperson and CEO of PepsiCo once said, "True success is being happy with yourself, is being fulfilled and that comes from devoting your time, your life, to doing what you love the most," Jack Welch's positive attitude towards people development in GEC became a driver for organizational change. Sachin Tendulkar, the great international cricket icon and legend once said that," My mood undergoes a change before every match as I start mentally preparing myself for winning and performing." A true example of optimistic and constructive attitude is that of Zaharias, champion in the 1932 Olympics and later a professional golfer. On one occasion, she penalised herself two strokes when she accidentally played the wrong ball. "Why did you do it?" asked a friend. "No one saw you. No one would have known the difference." "I would have known," Zaharias replied. Many corporate leaders have drawn their leadership lessons and inspiration from Vince Lombardi, one of America's most famous football coaches who wouldn't accept defeat as final. The stimulation for this was his consistent positive mind-set that broached through to reach his team's goal. In the corporate world, Southwest Airlines is not only an American icon but also the only major airline in the US that has been profitable. Its management works with a positive frame of mind and believes in promoting a supportive and enduring family-like culture that inspires its human resource to work with a captivating mind-set.

Formation of Attitudes

The main backbone of success is your attitude and not family background, education, intelligence, money or power, etc. A study conducted by sociologist Dr. Edward Banfield of Harvard University supports this. According to this, the main reason for **"success in life was a particular attitude of mind."** Attitudes and habits play a predominant role in the formulation of your mind-set. Attitudes in essence are your reflections to the outside world as it is a habitual response to situations surrounding you based on your thinking, mood and beliefs and reflect the state of your mind awareness. These are formed by your day to day experiences associated with the feelings as you go on in life. Some people often tend to believe that the negative statements are true and slowly these get registered in their subconscious mind and they get habituated in using these. Most people are unaware that by creating a negative atmosphere and impression may sound self-satisfying at that moment, but ultimately, it attracts negative energy only. If you start practising changing your thinking paradigms and beliefs, gradually these will become part of your overall mental makeup and start paying dividends. It is true that no one is perfect and therefore, no one has a perfect mind-set, but you can always work towards having a self-assured and constructive approach to your problems. According to Brian Tracy, "80 percent of your success as manager or as a salesperson will be determined by your attitude and only 20 percent by your aptitude." According to Cox Report, an in-depth study of Fortune 500 company executives revealed that over 90 percent of the executives attributed their business success to attitudes versus any other basic ingredient. **A study by Harvard University found that 85% of the time it is because of attitudes that one gets a job and only 15% of the time because of smartness, etc.**

Take a look at this story:

> *"Once while Buddha was teaching a group of people, he found himself on the receiving end of a fierce outburst of abuse from a bystander, who was for some reason very angry. The Buddha listened to the stranger's vented rage and then said to the group and to the stranger, "If someone gives a gift to another person, who then chooses to decline it, tell me, who would then own the gift- The giver or the person who refuses to accept the gift?" The giver," said the group after a little thought. "Any fool can see that," added the angry stranger." Then it follows, does it not," said the Buddha, "Whenever a person tries to abuse us, or to unload their anger on us, we can each choose to decline or to accept the abuse; whether to make it ours or not. By our personal response to the abuse from another, we can choose who owns and keeps the bad feelings."*(Excerpts: storiesfortrainers.com)

Changing the mind-set is no doubt a Herculean task, since it involves changing the self-behaviour. However, a focussed attempt, patience and practice over a period of time gradually pays. **You may often fail to appreciate that mind-set is basically your flexibility to situations in life.** You would have observed in your day to day people interaction, that heavens may fall, some people would continue with their inflexible attitudes and rigidity even if it leads to unhappiness and letdowns. Exactly, this is the type of outlook that you may need to alter while you embark on taking total charge of your success campaign.

Take a look at the following story:

> *"A farmer's old mule once tripped and fell into the well. The farmer heard the mule jarring and was unable to figure out how to bring up the old animal.*

It grieved him that he could not pull the animal out. Although the farmer sympathised with the mule, he called his neighbours and told them what had happened. He had them help haul dirt to bury the old mule in the well and quietly put him out of his misery. At first, the old mule was puzzled, but as the farmer and his neighbours continued shovelling and the dirt hit his back, he had a thought: he ought to shake off the dirt and step up. And he did just that. "Shake it off and step up...shake it off and step up...shake it off and step up." Even though, he took painful blows of dirt and fought panic, he just kept right on shaking it off and stepping up! It wasn't long before the old mule stepped up and over the lip of that well." *(Excerpts: storiesfortrainers.com)*

What could have buried and perished the old mule actually was a blessing in disguise. It all depends how you handle life's adversities and struggles- with calm senses or despair?

How to Build a Positive Mind-set

Changing to a constructive mind-set doesn't happen in isolation; it is a change in totality, i.e., changes of attitudes, thinking, feelings and conduct. It is being conscious of your actions and self-discipline and no doubt is a difficult proposition due to sheer affection with comfort in prevailing mind-set and habits and also facing resistance at the subconscious levels. At times, it appears as if you are sacrificing yourself from habits with which you have grown up. Developing and maintaining a constructive mind-set is an outcome of proactive behaviour and takes time, lot of practice, patience and commitment. You must remember that changing even few characteristics of your behaviour is a long drawn affair that requires working with a strong commitment, repeated practice and self-affirmations. It is like learning how to spell or use grammar or even practising mathematical problems by doing it over and over again.

1. Try Staying Mentally Fit

Like you give importance to your looks, conduct, attire and physical fitness, the same importance needs to be given to your mental fitness to remain responsive, flexible and unlocked. Initiate a process of self-coaching by absorbing and retrieving constructive thoughts that not only create a good aura around, but also boost your campaign. Look at impediments as a challenge and struggles and hindrances as opportunities to prove your mantel. Remaining upbeat with constructive perception helps your mind take a signal and slowly you will start creating positive manifestations around. Be patient as mind-sets don't change overnight. As said earlier, one needs to undertake gruelling practice on improving self-behaviour.

2. Focus on Thoughts and Feelings

Thought is a primary energy and a dynamic force and reflects your way of life, vehicle of *karma*, emotions and this makes or mars your destiny. Although we are born without any thoughts but we do pick up positive or negative thoughts from our parents, school and society and at times residual of our past *karmas* also. Thoughts, feelings and emotions are all interdependent. These shape each other and are an outcome of your mind-set. Every thought is a seed you plant. Positive seeds in time start reaping miracles for yourselves and make your dreams come true. No wonder as many as 60,000 thoughts traverse through our minds during the day knowingly or unknowingly. These are a mix of both positive and negative contents and are generally concerned with us and our immediate interests. **Research shows that about 80 percent thoughts**

belong to the past, 15 percent to the future and minuscule 5 percent to the present. When you change thoughts towards positive, there is bound to be a change in your vision, inner personality dynamics and choices in life. However, generally thoughts and internal conversations are negative and get reflected on your appearance and body language and need to be put under scanner every now and then. As soon as a negative thought comes into the mind, think for a moment whether it is going to be of any help in your personal elevation and overall effectiveness and can you earnestly try replacing it with a positive one. At first, this may look awkward and impractical because usually most people operate with a negative mind-set. Gradually, as feelings settle down, you will start feeling a little upbeat. Initiating change gradually to constructive ones, no doubt seems irrelevant and wastage of time to begin with. If you remain enduring and have the will to change, positive results start trickling slowly. No doubt it is practically impossible to keep yourself away all the time from the negative things around; yet you can try earnestly to focus on good and constructive things in the interest of being successful.

I am of the opinion that our mind on a mental plater is divided into two parts: the devilish (negative thoughts) and the angel (positive thoughts). Both these exist side by side, each trying to overpower the other. However, the devilish tendencies in your internal conversations may often win the battle of controlling most of your thoughts and feelings. Anger, ego, desire and greed are emotions which are the pillars of your devilish tendencies within. These emotions rock your mind, disturb it and ultimately lead you to failures, sufferings and frustrations. Remember you are here with a mission to accomplish your success campaign. Regardless of your life situations, you are the gardener of your own story. When you realise this, you will start creating only the best for yourself.

> *"Watch your thoughts, for they become words. Watch your words, for they become actions. Watch your actions, for they become habits. Watch your habits, for they become character. Watch your character, for it becomes your destiny."*
>
> **–Unknown**

3. Reframe Setbacks

Many times you may have trouble maintaining a constructive mind-set as often exterior events on which you have least control prompt negative and downbeat feelings. For example, driving to a seminar, you might become annoyed on facing a number of traffic jams and you immediately get into a bad frame of mind and construe as an awful day. As a result, you may walk to the seminar feeling depressed, frustrated and this may affect your performance at the seminar. Why become depressed, after all what control do you have on exterior events, such as traffic jams or other obstacles? Understand that exterior events are part of life and keep reminding the self every time you go through an obstacle. Once these events have a different meaning, there are less chances of triggering a bad mood.

4. Observe People with Positive Mind-set

Keep observing people with encouraging attitudes, amiable conduct and etiquettes keenly and make a mental note of it. Now stand before a mirror and copy what was observed like the way a person communicates, his/her body language, tone of speech, etc. Then couple this act with visualising as if you are doing what the person in question was doing and thinking in similar ways. Repeat this for few days. This gradually helps in acquiring some of the traits of the person you're modelling. Look at the people you admire and find what their personality traits and values are that are missing in you and plan how soon you can pick on these.

5. Avoid Negative Societal Interactions

Firstly, avoid interactions with those who depict downbeat conduct day in and day out. Such people are found every where criticizing, abusing and backbiting, etc. Restrict interactions to the bare minimum. Spend less time with those who discourage and are often found brushing shoulders and more with those, who make you feel good with their constructive outlook to life. Secondly, there may be an occasion when by designing negative situations are created at home/ work/ in relationships, etc. This may create a bad atmosphere around. Maintain cool and calm temper as far as possible and avoid direct participation by maintaining independent identity. If possible, shift from the situation. Remember a lotus plant grows in the mud and dirt and roses grow along with thorns. Both lotus and roses attract and are adored by one and all. For example,

> *The friends and colleagues you spend the most time around influence you whether you want them to or not! But there may be some one around with whom you have a small and occasional meeting, yet his power of influence may override the negative attitudes bombarding you. This individual may appear unassuming and unimpressive, yet may be thoroughly positive in all respects.*

6. Being Positive is a Choice, Grab it

Changing to a helpful and positive mind-set is not a license against facing failures, but surely your point of view starts changing when you are influenced by positive surroundings. This, no doubt becomes an important component of your success campaign. Sometimes, you may change attitudes temporarily because that becomes the need of the hour even though your mind may not concur. This is counter productive since good attitudes are not on switch on and switch off mode. Take a look:

> *"One evening an old man told his grandson about a battle that goes on inside People. He said, "My son, the battle is*

between two "wolves" inside us all. One is Evil. It is anger, envy, jealousy, sorrow, regret, greed, arrogance, self-pity, guilt, resentment, inferiority, lies, false pride, superiority and ego. The other is good. It is joy, peace, love, hope, serenity, humility, kindness, benevolence, empathy, generosity, truth, compassion and faith." The grandson thought about it for a minute and then asked his grandfather, "Which wolf wins?" The old man replied, "The one you feed.""

7. Constructive Mind-set Begins from Home

Accomplishments and letdowns are temporary phases in your life but mind-set is your life companion in whatever state of affair you are in and needs servicing every now and then by carrying an unbiased assessment periodically. Like discipline starts from self, initiate change in self before expecting children, colleagues, friends and others to bring in changes. Maintaining time schedules, viz. being on time to work, meetings, appointments and meeting deadlines at work depicts attitude towards your work ethics.

8. Negativities Affect Emotional Health

Some people unfortunately feel below dignity to bend and pick good attitudes. Sometimes, I observe people in power, arrogant individuals, autocratic superiors or even older people commenting, 'Listen to me' or 'Do what I say' and pressurise people with their opinions which often leads to bad blood. **Bringing elasticity in your thinking and approach is the foundation of positive mind-set**. People who don't change direction and keep up with the time not only lose in accomplishing their goals, but are labelled as-egoistic, having locked minds, least concern for others' feelings and are by and large, not liked. More often than not, such conduct not only blocks effective communications but also affects teamworking. Try to bring flexibility by having an unbolted mind, encourage open communication channels, believe in give and take and develop taking a balanced view of situations. **Learn to use head and heart in a balanced proportion to develop likable attitudes.**

Understand that by bowing and curving, you don't become small, in fact, you raise your opinion and respect among people. Learn to accept mistakes and apologies for the same by heart and not for namesake say, 'Sorry.' It manures your positive thinking and brushes up your attitudes.

9. Be Hopeful

Constructive and hopeful mind-set ensures that you stay confident in whatever you do. Remember that a hopeful invariably becomes successful in achieving the mission because of his sheer emphasis on being upbeat and positive even in distress. Hopefuls have a habit of developing an attitude of keep learning to be affirmative, self-motivated and seeing good in people and not finding faults and weaknesses. For example, "I will not meet my work target this year because my teammates play politics behind me and do not cooperate in work." Stop and turn this negative thought into something like this: "I and my team always do the best and my commitment to achieving yearly work targets will reap great rewards for the team, and in turn for the company."

10. Power of Communication

Frequently complaining about situations, cribbing every now and then, talking ill or passing sarcastic remarks are some harmful traits commonly found in most? This develops negativities and affects your mind-set. Secondly, there are occasions, when you feel unhappy and frustrated because of bad conduct of people. At times, you may be tempted to hit back. Try to maintain calm and just react by a smile. Build power of digesting such ill-mannered conduct. Constructive thinking patterns and feelings call for useful expressions. For example, don't use negative phrases, such as **"I can't," "It's impossible," "This won't work" or "I don't care, get lost," etc**. What you communicate reflects what is already in your mind-set. Think before communicating by evaluating words because what you communicate once can't be retrieved.

Summing up...

Imagine if you had a subordinate, who was always found depicting depressing conduct, would you recommend his elevation? You would expect the individual to first reform his conduct. Gaining altitude and achieving accomplishments in life primarily is pushiness and above all, an upbeat mind-set. **There is no readymade formula to success, you have to first conquer vices within, rearm with positives before starting to work on your campaign.** No half-hearted approach will work nor will unplanned moves succeed. Try working on attitudes by assessing feelings and beliefs and tame these to positives by repeated practice. Twitter within and just observe the internal conversations. Most of these are negative and destructive. You have a challenge to conquer within your mind-set before you proceed further.

How to Build a Tough Mental Attitude

Having understood the important role a balanced mind-set plays in accomplishing your success campaign, you next need to take steps to build a tough and resilient mind. Don't feel helpless, hopeless and solutionless. Over and over again, most of you scratch head and feel, **"Why I have failed. I never expected. I really don't know what went wrong. I am in total disarray."** But imagine if there were no crisis and everything was smooth sailing, would success be boneless? **A real success, undoubtedly is like peeling an onion. By precisely removing each layer of outer onion, you are able to appreciate the complexities at each level as you eventually reach the core – achieving your success campaign.** While managing upheavals, why do some of you stick it out while others don't? Because others possibly haven't harnessed their mental and physical stamina nor have they learnt how to stay put and hang on to withstand failure and disappointments. They feel offended, keep cursing their luck, but don't look at themselves and find what they lack to improve. **Stamina is the test of your boldness and internally generated potency that allows to remain in saddle and keep going to the finishing line, no matter how long it takes and how difficult the task is**. After all, every boat stays afloat in an unruffled ocean; the real stay put of a boat is known when the ocean roars and thunders. I always communicate in my training workshops that, **when the goal gets tougher, the**

tougher gets resilient. I am reminded of following Aesop's tortoise and the hare story.

> *True to its nature, the hare ran fast, while the tortoise was slow but persistent, and no way could keep up with the hare. After a while, he passed the place where the hare had stopped to take a snooze while the determined tortoise continued grazing down the path. The hare woke up and continued speeding towards the finish line. Meanwhile, the tortoise had already crossed the finish line just ahead of the hare. Surprisingly, the hare should have won the race, but that was not true. Taking a cue from this story, the fast and the strong do not always win – only because they quit even if it is for a short period of time.*

Moral of the story: The tortoise had a persistent and determined mind. He did appear slow but was consistent, determined, persistent and staying put with his resolute.

With resilience, patience and ability to hang around, you can cross over failure and accomplish success as was done by the tortoise. Your mental and physical stamina, doggedness, will to hang around and resistance is all that makes you stick and be unyielding, while most pack and retreat. Mental and physical stamina doesn't take place automatically, you have to be mentally and physically fit, be committed and maintain patient and a cool head.

> *"Success in life depends upon staying in power. The reason for failure in most cases is lack of perseverance. Men get tired and give up."*
>
> *– J.R. Miller*

Just peep in the immediate past and recall when something didn't go your way, did you tend to bounce back or fell apart? Resilience, staying around and stamina is not a supernatural force to ward off your failure. But these surely give strength, confidence and power to rebound from failure and handle stress out of disappointments better. Power of stamina means adapting to the nuisances of failure and keeping ready punches to strike back. It also means keeping your psychological, emotional and physical state active and somewhat agile. No doubt, low feelings are natural to occur on a failure. But those with tough mental attitude are resilient enough and cope within no time. They are well aware that they have to travel height and distance to conquer failure. Ultimately, what helps sticking is the will to keep the flame within afire and undeterred, commitment to build skills to endure hardship. Resilience is also an evolving process that can be honed and strengthened over time.

> *"Nothing in this world can take the place of persistence. Talent will not; nothing is more common than unsuccessful people with talent. Genius will not; unrewarded genius is almost a proverb. Persistence and determination alone are omnipotent. The slogan "press on" has solved and always will solve the problems of the human race."*
>
> *– Calvin Coolidge*

Guidelines to Build Stamina and Resilience

Learning to build mental and physical stamina is an on going process and doesn't build overnight. It is a sustained process and takes place gradually once you face problems and disappointments and resolve these satisfactorily. Do not have unrealistic expectations and become intolerant on delays. Remember behind each success; lies months of practice, mock presentations and experimentations. For example, a clay potter probably has several earthenwares in his collection that will never be seen. Therefore, just practise! Coach Bear Bryant said once that, **"What matters is not the size of the dog in the fight, but the size of the fight in the dog."**

1. Build on Physical and Mental Energy

Good mental and physical energy levels help in bearing hardships and catalyses firmness to remain focussed and tough. How pushy you have made yourselves to tackle obstacles and problems determines the level of stamina you have developed. **Persistence is an opportunity in the worst of scenarios and stimulus, push and pull**. Do not make gloomy comments about self and avoid describing the self as a letdown even under extreme provocation or aggravation and keep the tone of voice upbeat. This keeps the stamina going by making you internally strong, confident, unwavering and hard-wearing to relaunch your samurai ambush on success campaign. (For details, see chapter 14.)

The following tips will be of help:

- ❑ Changing lifestyle habits helps in energising mind, stabilising moods, improving alertness and focus. As said earlier, get adequate rest by having 7-8 hours of sleep each night with periodical periods of relaxation during the day. Spend half an hour in the neighbourhood park in the morning hours and focus your mind and senses to the enchanting environment, observe the immediate surroundings, people, their behaviour, expressions, etc.
- ❑ Eating a healthy and nutritious diet. Solid nutrition is a key element in increasing mental stamina. Like other parts of your body, the mind needs certain key nutrients in order to function at the peak performance. Avoid processed sugars, eat enough protein and iron and consume plenty of water.
- ❑ Mental exercises such as crossword puzzles, chess, playing cards, observing what is happening in the moment, etc. helps your mind develop sharpness and concentration.

2. Stop Contemplating

Keep a watch on how you react and respond to various distress and painful situations in life by accepting that changes and stressful events are part of your success campaign. Alter the way you interpret challenges and adversities. Instead of seeing these as unsolvable problems, see these as opportunities for improvement. Secondly, practise coping with different kinds of situations you face every day by paying attention. You may also like to consult seniors at work or others who you feel have strong power of resilience and seek their advice for further improvement. With each instance of dealing with challenges, improve on the time you take to cope with it. This way you will be in a better state to handle sudden adverse situations.

3. Sense of Purpose

Some time you may not be clear about your purpose and campaign. For example, just saying, "I want to be successful" is not at all sufficient. Therefore, define the purpose threadbare to send cues to your mind. The stronger your sense of purpose, the better equipped you are to handle challenges and setbacks and to recover from them. Any lack of clarity will only lead to further problems and frustrations. Being able to identify your purpose in detail and in depth can help you feel that you are on the right track and have a meaningful purpose.

4. Dust of Negative Thoughts

Failure is distress and disappointment, and produces mental crisis that often lead to negative internal dialogues making you feel shaky and insecure. But the characteristic of a resilient mind is not to lose hope or become demotivated and unenthusiastic. Just get up, dust off the psyche and look at the situation from a different viewpoint to put a positive turn around. Focus the mind on your self-belief that you desire success hard enough, no matter how difficult and unattainable it may seem. Operate from an optimistic and flexible set of beliefs and soon situation is bound to change for the better. Use affirmations to turn thoughts to a positive approach. Resilient people see challenge, not threat and each struggle they overcome is not only a challenge but a life lesson, and this strengthens their mental stamina and power to hang around. Remember, that in order to be successful, you must be hundred percent convinced that you are going to be successful with your success campaign come what may. (For details, read chapter 20.)

5. Don't see Crisis as Unmanageable

Plan, gear up and take decisive actions rather than keeping aloof or shirking away and thinking obstacles would vanish away automatically with the time. Each situation comes up with a message, so understand and learn from it. You can't change, delay or escape from adverse situations or disappointments on a failure, but you can change how you understand and counter these events. Confidence in your ability to solve problems and believing your gut feeling and impulse helps build mental stamina and firmness in hanging out.

6. Be Flexible to Bend

As said earlier, flexibility in approach, practical thinking patterns, helpful feelings and an attitude of bending are the hallmark of improving on your mental stamina and staying power. Understand the thinking patterns and if change is required, try altering these so that pressures can be handled well and you are able to spring back from hold ups and hindrances. Bending is primarily a personality characteristic, and is generally an outcome of your ego levels and attitudes. Can you ask someone to give a fair run down on your attitudes and thinking paradigm so that you can work on the feedback?

7. Emotional Considerations

Positive or negative emotions are an outcome of your thinking style. On a failure, your emotions are first to get affected and your ability to manage, control and respond appropriately helps to stay calm under pressure and fear. It is useful to spend some time in assessing emotions and their variations if any, and suitably modifying these depending on individual personality dynamics. Positive and controlled emotions are going to be important partners on the success campaign and for mental and physical well-being. As said earlier, it is must for you to pay attention to your feelings and emotions. Indulge in activities that you enjoy and find relaxing. Read the success stories of people who succeeded against all odds.

8. Social Support

Research has consistently demonstrated that strong relationships are a key resilience factor. Surround yourself with like-minded people. It is important to interact with constructive people who will complement, are motivated and goal-oriented and are resilient enough.

CHAPTER 15

Road Map to Goal Setting

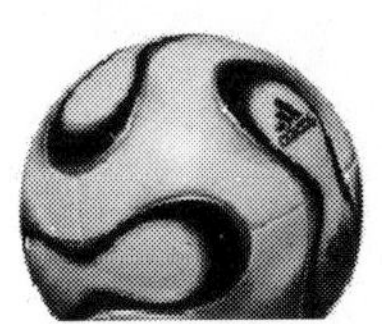

Having made up your mind to be hard-wearing and tough to accomplish your success campaign, the next step is to understand the importance of goal setting and how to go about it. Let me share a story briefly. 'Alice in Wonderland', a famous novel written by Lewis Carrol tells of a story of a girl named Alice who falls down a rabbit hole into a fantasy world- Wonderland populated by peculiar creatures. In a dialogue with the caterpillar, she inquires, "Excuse me, Sir," "Could you tell me which road to take?" Wisely, the caterpillar asks, "Where are you going?" Somewhat dismayed, Alice responds, "Oh, I don't know where I am going, Sir." "Well," replied the caterpillar, "if you don't know where you are going, it really doesn't matter which road you take."

This is exactly what happens when you are not goal specific on your success campaign. Most of you fail in your success campaign because you perhaps don't appreciate that realistic goals are the single most important factor. A strict adherence to goals calls for undergoing a process of self-change which very few find appealing. This is the state of affair of goal setting in lives of most people; no wonder most of you spend a goalless life, yet may have number of achievements more by default than by design. French writer Antoine de Saint-Exupery once said that, **"A goal without a plan is just a wish."** The analogy from this quote is that the goal needs to be backed by your inner desire and passion that drives you to accomplishment. When you plan to rebuild from ground zero, you are expected to be pushy and achievement-oriented that often helps in meeting the success campaign. Initially, this may appear difficult but as your feelings normalise signs of upbeat start showing. While your goals need to be specific, at the same time these need to be realistic and achievable. For example, don't set big goals like losing ten kilos of weight in a month. Instead, translate what that means into what you're going to do on a day-to-day basis.

Review Goals and Actions

Often failure takes place due to lack of consistent efforts, commitments, risk taking abilities and looking for shortcuts. It is inevitable to make an unbiased self-enquiry on the causes, such as: whether failure was due to insufficient preparation, missing on complete focus or lack of appropriate action? The feedback generated so helps in deciding a revised and improved plan of action. Questions, such as: "What is that I need to do? Is there a need for putting in additional efforts? Do I need outside consultation/help? Do I require more practice/learning, etc.?" Reviewing the goal and action to attain it will always be at the centre stage. Review essentially includes the following:

- Were the priorities in the right order?
- Was the road map and action plan right? Can I review it?
- Were deadlines realistic or not?
- Were there any problems faced in implementing the action plan?
- Were reviews carried out periodically to make additions/alterations, etc.?

Working on your goal and being committed is always going to be tiresome, but what matters most is your dedication to the ultimate objective that helps to carryout your goal to its accomplishment.

Guidelines to Goal Setting

1. Clarity of Goal

Goal requires clarity, specificity in nature and should be to the point in characteristics. For instance, you are working as a manager and getting reasonably good salary, but you are not able to save or buy some luxuries. You start feeling that if you had more money, you will do this and you will do that. Therefore, your objective becomes having and saving more money. Having more money is a goal that seems very vague and general in nature. You need to be specific and ask yourself: How much more money, how will you go about it and how long will it take you to achieve this. The more questions you ask yourself, the clearer your goal becomes. Once you know the exact outcome of your goal, you will be able to create an action plan. The emphasis in goal setting is on 'conceiving' and 'believing'. Conceiving translates to formulation of clear and specific goals, while believing leads to self-assurance in achieving the goal. For example, Australian psychologist Alan Richardson conducted a study about basketball players. He selected three groups of players. One was to practise shooting free throws 20 minutes a day, the second was to do none at all and the third to visualise getting baskets for 20 minutes a day. The group that practised improved 23%, and the group that did nothing, did not improve at all. However, the group that visualised also showed a 23% improvement.

Define the purpose and the desired outcome of what you want to achieve and what you need to forfeit for it. When you have a specific idea in mind, it becomes easier to draw the road map to accomplishing your success campaign. How fast you get to your goal depends on the strength of your purpose, self-worth and flexibility to adjust to a new situation. For example, a soldier's one-point goal is always focussed on how to install his country's flag across the border should there be a war. To tap it, goal formulated needs to be:

1. **Specific**: Concrete, expressed in positive terms and to the point.

2. **Measurable:** System to evaluate progress and whether you are on the right track.
3. **Achievable:** Whether required resources are in place?
4. **Realistic:** Whether practical? Unrealistic goals are just dreams and figures of imagination.
5. **Timely:** Setting deadlines for completion and sticking to it.
6. **Reversals:** Keep provisions for temporary failures/ reversals, be open for feedback.

2. Formulating Action Plan

Goal setting needs to be supported by a well-defined action plan giving the time frame and how you will go about it. Generally, most failures are neither clear about their goal nor an action plan. The goal is often in their mind playing a see-saw game and is rarely shown the light of the day. There is lot to learn from the wisdom of Napoleon Hill and become wiser, **"When defeat comes, accept it as a signal that your plans are not sound, rebuild those plans, and set sail once more towards your coveted goal."** Formulating a strategy on action assumes importance since most often actions do not commensurate with what all goes in achieving the success campaign. No action will succeed unless meticulously planned taking into account even minute details, pitfalls, problems, etc. The following steps will be useful:

- ❑ Put down all actions/options step by step. Evaluate their feasibility keeping resources, such as time in mind.
- ❑ Prioritise the steps by their importance and effectiveness? After setting a definite goal, identify the worries and doubts that usually surround a failure.

  Look at these with concern and decide how to get rid of these.
- ❑ Monitor execution of plan, make adjustments and review progress at each step.
- ❑ Don't do everything at once. Take smaller steps by breaking down the goal into smaller goals.

- Once the plan is ready for implementation, start taking one step at a time.

3. Review and Evaluation

It is important to periodically review the progress. Establish key areas where improvements may be necessary. However, often subconsciously you tend to forget or neglect a continuous review of your performance on a set scale. Assessing the progress of your success campaign periodically helps to make small adjustments that in turn make achievements easier.

4. Be Prepared to take Risks

Sometimes fear of rejection, criticism and lack of risk taking ability holds some of you back from setting goals and a plan of action to achieve these. No accomplishment in life is possible unless you are prepared to undergo the risk of failure and sometimes may be repeatedly. Albert Bandura, a psychologist from Stanford University, defined self-efficacy as a 'belief in your own ability to succeed and your ability to achieve the goals you set for yourselves'. This belief pays dividends when planning a goal and has an enormous force on your approach to goal setting and your choices.

5. Ensure key Links are in Place

Sometimes key links in attainment of your campaign are missing and some of you may not be clear what you desire and how to kickstart. Elements such as: planning, formulating, operations, focus are all essential prerequisites to achieving your success goal. For example, Tom Watson, the founder of IBM was once asked what the reasons of phenomenal success of IBM were. He said it was 1) Creating a very clear image in his mind of what he wanted his company to look like when it was done. 2) How a company like that has to act on a day-to-day basis. 3) In the very beginning of building his company, he began to act in that way.

How to Stay Focussed

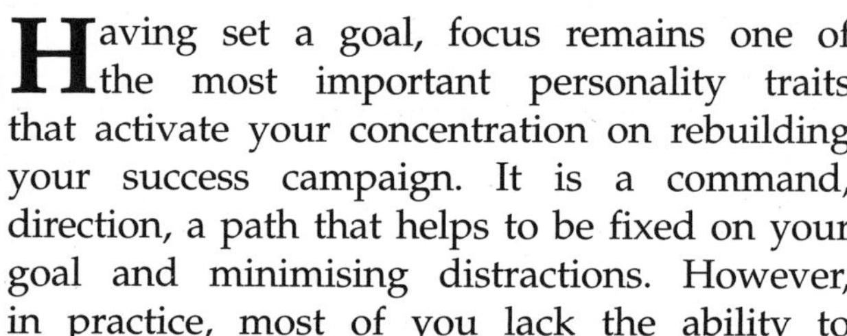

Having set a goal, focus remains one of the most important personality traits that activate your concentration on rebuilding your success campaign. It is a command, direction, a path that helps to be fixed on your goal and minimising distractions. However, in practice, most of you lack the ability to focus on your campaign resulting in underperformance or delay in achieving accomplishment. Success is an outcome of seriousness in formulating realistic goals and being extremely focussed while these are under execution. No campaign is worth its salt, if you don't have a strong push for formulating and executing it, and also if it is not backed by the inner strength and firmness. On a failure, sometimes you do not realise that harsh conditions and challenges often lead to resolution and strength of intellect when you are under constant threat for survival. It is in such or similar situations, you become tough, resolute and self-enthused to focus on the campaign that is your endurance and survival. Sometimes, failing and underperformance fuels the desire that drives you to be extremely focussed to achieve your success campaign even if the path you have to travel may be full of bumps and knocks. If you happen to watch athletes keenly, you will be amazed to see how focussed they are on their goals and use it in outshining in the competitions. They use their mental skills and psyche to create attentiveness and self-assurance.

Focussing always remains a challenge. Some of you though good in concentration, fail to focus the moment they are asked to concentrate on something else. Your reflexes may be poor and as such, may have difficulty in not able to 'switch on and switch off.' Those who are able to focus intensely and in turn perform exceptionally are referred to as being 'In Flow'— a state of complete absorption with the activity at hand and the situation. However, in practice complete absorption in what you are doing becomes at times impossible because of constant distractions you face. Some times multi-tasking at work/home becomes an impediment to continuing with concentration and absorption. The Zen technique of mindfulness advocates one thing at a time- 'cook while you cook, read while you read.'

Guidelines for Improving on Focussing

1. Improve on Mental Picture

Mental picture is a process which enables you to observe, think, imagine and take appropriate steps to convert and implement your ideas and actions for the attainment of your success campaign. It is an art of developing new ideas by making gainful use of your mind energy. Develop an attitude and habit for visualisation by looking at things in different perspectives, by generating passion, perseverance, patience and an inquisitive mind. Visualise mentally pictures of success and focus the mind to explore new paths, new thinking and experimentation. The best time for visualisation is in the morning. Close your eyes and for the next 5-10 minutes, dream how to work on your success campaign to inspire and self- motivate. As a part of daily routine, spare some time and focus your mind and senses to enchanting images, such as the sound of running water, chirping of birds, whistling of the cool breeze, ringing of the temple/church bells or chanting of prayers. Listening to music or watching the miracles of nature helps in developing attitude for creative imagination and also smoothes the body and mind nerves.

2. Power of Attention

Concentration means that you can focus on one thing by having a strong, alert and focussed mind. Attainment of your campaign becomes comparatively easy if you are able to utilise the good constructive thoughts and shun away the distractive ones. Through concentration, you are able to hold your mental power to your specific objective and not allow wavering or focussing on disturbing thoughts. Take a look at the following story:

> *Once a fisherman could not catch fish the whole day and it started getting dark. But he kept trying, holding the net tight in his hands, ready to pull it up, when a stranger approached him. "Sir," "can you tell me where the Letterman's live?" There was no reply from the fisherman as he was just on the verge of pulling up his rod. The stranger repeated his request in a louder voice, "Sir, can you tell me where the Letterman's live?" But the fisherman was seriously engrossed in catching the fishes and seemed unaware of everything around him. The stranger felt annoyed and thus continued walking. Suddenly, the fisherman caught a big fish and he turned and shouted "Hey!" "'Come here! Listen! But the stranger continued walking. After much shouting, however, he did come back. "What did you ask me about?" said the fisherman. "Why, I repeated my question so many times and here you are, asking me to repeat it again!" The fisherman replied: "At that time a fish was after my bait, so I didn't hear a word of what you said."*

Moral

While concentrating, you must be completely absorbed and focussed to achieve the desired results.

Following guidelines will be useful for developing concentration:

1. Learn by practice to visualise your success campaign and then set the mind faculties on achieving it and not shift the focus.

2. Practise being an attentive and active listener. Listening requires patience and you can't concentrate unless you are habituated with patience. Work on patience and tolerance skills.
3. Try to keenly observe a thought for some time. This way you set a pitch for developing skills in concentration. Your senses transmit appropriate messages which get converted in to set of thoughts and are analysed by your mind. When you concentrate on a person/situation, it absorbs your whole thought and you start developing concentration skills. Care needs to be taken to concentrate on positive aspects only because it is the habit of mind to get attracted to negativities.
4. When you put your mind energy to attention, you are able to put your total faculties of mind to a singular path. This can be done by focussing your total concentration on to the focal point of your campaign.
5. As said earlier, regular breathing exercise, i.e. inhaling and exhaling deep breaths from your nostrils and observing the inhaling and exhaling helps in augmenting concentration gradually.
6. Inculcate the habit of one task at a time. This is mindfulness. You can also spend 5-10 minutes in the morning by keeping silent, closing eyes and allowing thoughts to come, watch and go. No attachment with the thoughts. But your concentration on breathing should continue unabated.
7. Ask your spouse/friend to be a speaker. Go to a room free from TV/Phone/other distractions. Ask the speaker to write down a paragraph of his choice which is not known to you. Let the speaker read out in normal speed. You keep listening carefully with full attention. Once the speech is finished, start writing what you heard and then compare. Increase the difficulty and length of speech and write. Now start remembering what is being read. Don't write

just remember and then speak what you heard. Repeatedly do this exercise for next couple of days. Initially, you may feel irritated but as you go along, you would realise improvements and after few weeks, you would have improved substantially on your concentration skills.

3. Think of the Finish Line

It helps to think of the ultimate destination/desire as it not only sustains your interest, but also increases the focussing power.

4. Encouraging Ideas

Focussing requires attentiveness and assimilation which is only possible if unconstructive thoughts are not traversing through your mind. These not only disturb your focus but equally undermine your performance, interpersonal relations, creative ideas, decision making and work output, etc. Therefore self-generate positive orientations both within and outside before you start concentrating and getting absorbed. Remember focussing means positive mind-set. For instance:

- The USP of athletes and other sportspersons is their positive state of mind. They manage nervousness if any with relaxation techniques and maintain constant concentration while they are performing during competitions.
- Good candidates approach the interview selection panel with a confident and positive state of mind. Their minds generally are relaxed. They concentrate and remain absorbed about their abilities and performing well. They don't get distracted with outcome.

5. Building Staying Power

As said earlier, learn how athletes build on their mental and physical power. They are usually found pushing past the point of their tiredness and frustration and end up building their mental toughness. The incentive schemes in business and industry serves as an example here. Increasing numbers in manufacturing/selling output makes employees earn extra within their normal duty hours by focussing on putting extra efforts. (For details, see chapter14.)

6. Develop Strategies

Often delays and obstacles in achieving your success campaign lead to losing focus and getting derailed. To overcome such setbacks, it is important to have strategies in place to tackle such and similar issues. Sometimes, delays help in refocussing or carrying out adjustments. Setbacks and frustrations are common part of success campaign. Be prepared. If nothing works, step back and look for solutions from intuitions or consult friends.

Work on your Optimism Levels

Goal setting and being focussed on your success campaign will not take off unless you develop being optimistic and hopeful of accomplishing your campaign. No one is born with either an optimistic or pessimistic behaviour although in some cases, traces may be in one's genes. It is a behaviour that one learns through self-generating experiences or being motivated by others like *"You are resilient or you are a winner, you are a loser or you are useless, etc."* Remember optimism will always remain an anchor in building your self-confidence and make you self-assured when working on your challenges. But at times, some of you feel pessimistic and distrustful because of the negative experiences generated due to the fear of failure and unfound apprehensions. Being pessimistic puts your mind space to imaginary scenarios and removes your focus from managing challenges to accomplish your goals. Apprehensions and panic in a way are also well-knitted in your mind by past unfavourable events and situations. Optimism or pessimism are behaviours that are picked up as we go on in our lives through our day to day life experiences and people interactions. But surely over a period of time, motivation and encouragement helps change from pessimistic behaviour to optimistic one. Psychologists have studied the correlation between thoughts and beliefs on our behaviour and conduct. They have found out that the way people reason with themselves about various things in their lives has a huge brunt on their success campaign. Studies have shown that naysayer and pessimists are up to eight times more likely to become depressed when bad events occur.

If Thomas Edison had taken to fears after hundreds of failures, I guess mankind would still be in the age of candle light and lanterns. Jack Welch, Bill Gates, Richard Branson, Donald Trump, Steve Jobs, Sam Walton, Rattan Tata, Narayan Murthi, Sunil Mittal and several others will always be remembered for their fearless business leadership in spite of stiff opposition. They motivated and inspired thousands whose attempts to succeed didn't materialise in the first go. Whenever you decide to take the fear head on by facing and accepting it, you initiate positive and optimistic steps to remove apprehensions and doubts about accomplishing your goal. Rarely one can find individuals who have the courage not to fear the failure. If you garner a mind-set that, "whatever I undertake in life, there are chances of failure as there are for success," you move ahead with a relatively free mind. It is also true that at times being pessimistic may be beneficial. According to Psychological research, some times pessimistic behaviour may be useful, especially if you happen to take a higher risk in life, it may ring the caution bell to make you alert and think twice.

Martin Seligman, Director, Positive Psychology Center at the University of Pennsylvania and a past President of the American Psychological Association has demonstrated the differences in people who become depressed and those who do not, based on the kinds of attributions people make during difficult experiences. According to his research findings, "The defining characteristic of pessimists is that they tend to believe that bad events will last a long time, will undermine everything they do, and are their own fault. The optimists, who are confronted with the same hard knocks of this world, think about misfortune in the opposite way. They tend to believe that defeat is just a temporary setback or a challenge, that its causes are just confined to this one case." You are well aware that bad and unhappy events are part of life irrespective of whether you are pessimistic or optimistic. The only difference lies with your attitude, mind-set and self-talk about these events. An optimistic, resilient and positively oriented person is able to steer his way out of the crisis. What made many business leaders, entrepreneurs and political leaders great was their resilience, constructive and optimistic thinking. Greats such as Walt Disney, Henry Ford, Nelson Mandela, Karsanbhai Patel of Nirma fame, Ray Kroc of McDonald's, Sam Walton of Walmart, Kishore Biyani of Pantaloon Retail, Sumner M. Redstone of Viacom and thousands others never gave up living optimistically and thinking constructive, while they faced tough challenges to be where they reached. Imagine repeated failures and disappointments of Abraham Lincoln, Sir Winston Churchill fighting for public offices. The above given few illustrious names of individuals were all offsprings of optimism, sanguine, hopefulness and had never a say die attitude. The story goes that Thomas Edison was known for his positive attitude towards life. One day Edison was in the process of inventing his incandescent lamp. The headache in this process was to find a suitable material that glows on heating. He was trying a lot of combinations to suite his need but in vain(it is a pity tungsten was not popular in those days). But Edison was optimistic and not going to give up. However, his assistant was not as optimistic as him. One fine day, the assistant asked Edison with total loss of hope, what on earth he was trying to do and how does he intend to find the right substance in this way? Edison replied, "By checking these hundreds of compounds, I have eliminated the substances that do not glow. So I would soon be able to find the right substance in this way."

You must have felt at times a positive energy within spurs and makes you rearing to go all out to work and to accomplish your objective. This is the outcome of belief in yourself derived from being forceful and persistent on getting what you want. Leaders in different professions are admired for their optimistic mind-set that makes them stand out tall and be counted. A high level of optimism is a great motivator and not only inspires self-reliance around, but is a confirmed ticket for you on a flight to success. But the process doesn't end with getting success; you need to analyse your thoughts, strengths, actions and beliefs and what role these played in your missions accomplished. This way you are not only self-assuring about your optimistic bent of mind, but also creating a base for managing for future challenges with grit and unyielding mind. For instance, say to yourself that I have a flat to live rather than saying I don't have a bungalow to stay or self-branding is extremely difficult instead say and feel that "I have grit and competencies, I shall be a brand one day." This way you are not only separating yourself from negative thinking but strengthening your resolve by sending positive strokes to your mind. For instance, Ray Kroc, founder of McDonald's once said that, "I was 52 years old. I had diabetes and incipient arthritis. I had lost my gall bladder and most of my thyroid gland in earlier campaigns, but I was convinced that the best was ahead of me." This is how great people take impediments in life head on by their optimistic mind-set and steadfastness. It would be pertinent to quote Zig Ziglar, author, salesman and a great motivational speaker that, **"It's your attitude and not your aptitude that determines your altitude."**

Guidelines to Become Optimistic

1. Dynamics of Your Traits

Some of you are too sensitive, impatient and emotional and have immediate and rash reaction to disappointments. They often feel negative on the spur of moment than others, who remain relatively calm, unfazed and take problems in stride. No doubt this may be part of their personality dynamics patterned at birth and may also be genetic, but you have the power to mould these to optimism by practising focussing on positive aspects of your life. Temperaments can be altered by changing your conduct, habits and tuning your mind to be open and flexible. Reactions can be minimised and changes incorporated by practice and paying attention to your self-talk. Learn from athletes who lose several times, yet keep calm and try their best to beat the competition.

2. Accept Things which Cannot be Changed

You may like to fight the odds to sail against the current. Sensing that the current is life threatening, you may at the spur of the moment decide to follow the current and re strategise on your countdown. What I am saying is that to win the war, be prepared to lose a few battles and learn from the experience. Acceptance in such situations turns your mind to optimism and reduces stress considerably. What is needed is appreciating the situation, looking at the available options, being positive about future course of events and putting your best to accomplish your desired goal.

3. Build on your Constructive Attitudes

Attitudes are habitual response to situations surrounding you based on your thinking, mood and beliefs with respect to your day to day experiences and play a predominant role in the formulation of your mind-set. Your attitudes also have a strong bearing on your optimism and physical energy levels that help in bearing hardships and catalyses firmness to remain focussed and tough. Do not make gloomy comments about the self and avoid describing the self as a letdown even under extreme provocation or aggravation and keep the tone of voice upbeat. Also your constructive outlook to life improves your quality of life. According to the research findings of Mayo Clinic, optimists live longer, have an impact on their quality of life and report a higher level of physical and mental well-being than pessimists. Dr. Toshihiko Maruta of Mayo Clinic reports that, "The wellness of being is not just physical, but attitudinal. How you perceive, what goes on around you and how you interpret it may have an impact on your longevity, and it could affect the quality of your later years." (Reference: sciencedaily.com/releases/2002)

4. Change Dynamics of Internal dialogues

It is the habit of human mind to keep alive to chattering, analysing and evaluating events, interpersonal communications, and non-verbal communications that we may or may not be a party. Most of the time internal dialogues are unconstructive, such as: being critical, reflecting unfounded fears, revengeful, anger, depressing, pessimistic, etc. However, at times, it may be constructive and creative. Negative internal dialogues usually end up making us disappointed, pessimistic and unenthusiastic. Therefore, what is needed is to try and internalise positive and constructive thoughts. For instance, you can think like, "I am wasting too much of my mind energy in frivolous, unnecessary and uncalled for thoughts. It appears that I am carrying lot of useless past information resulting in all sorts of confusion, conflicts, and I am not able to focus on my immediate goal. Can I get rid of these by deflecting the mind from focussing on these?" If you are able to induct small changes, much of your problems will start becoming simplified. When you internalise positive feelings through affirmations, you take a step forward for being optimistic and proactive conduct. Secondly, you can shift your thinking patterns and perception about others' situation without knowing the actual facts or reasons of behaving in a particular way which may be or not acceptable to you. Often going by perception, you are seeing others situations with a spectacle. Therefore changing perception to the reality helps in changing your attitudes based on perception to the reality and helps raise optimism levels. For instance, "A man and his kids boarded the train, and while his kids were yelling and throwing things around, he just sat there doing nothing. It was clear that everyone in the train was irritated, and when he couldn't take it anymore, Stephen Covey turned to the man and asked if he could control his kids. The man apologised and explained that he was feeling at a loss because the kids' mother died in hospital just an hour ago. " (Ref: Stephen R. Covey's '7 Habits of Highly Effective People')

5. Positive Occurrences

Develop the habit of viewing disappointments and negative events as temporary by practising and saying to you that if positive and constructive events have not lasted long, this disappointment or letdown too shall pass. You must develop the habit of switch on and switch off when trying to change the self-behaviour. If you are able to practise, you are well on road to optimism.

6. Flexible and Non-rigid Attitudes

Flexibility in your thinking and approach is usually a preface to an optimistic behaviour. Take a look at the following helpful steps:

- ❑ Improve on tolerance, fortitude, firmness and grit. Self-assessment and carrying suitable corrections gradually works. Start from home and make notes each time we are unbendable and think how you could get over this problem.
- ❑ Control emotions by being practical and having a professional outlook and also by disciplining the mind. Ask your spouse or friend to act as an auditor. One would improve gradually and feel satisfied when people observe change. Keep practising and enjoy being optimistic.

7. Positive self-made Norms of Responding to People and Situations

The starting point in any behavioural adjustment is to believe that you have the will and commitment to self-improvement and also assessing and observing your beliefs. Good and bad posture is an outcome of your thinking. It is entirely your choice to dust your mind and convert it to your advantage by repeated practice and affirmations.

8. Gear up Self-motivation and Self-confidence

High levels of self-confidence and self-motivation makes you internally strong. Actions and affirmative intent not only build an aura of positivism, but also bring in favourable circumstances that help in being optimistic. Unfortunately, unconstructive people are masters in creating problems rather than solving these and purposefully lend a deaf ear to remaining optimistic. They would prefer to suffer and suffocate but not change their thinking paradigms.

CHAPTER 18

Build on Self-Confidence

By now you would have got stimulated and charged up, self-assured and rearing to take off on your success campaign. This is the outcome of your self-confidence derived from being assertive on getting what you want. However, should you lack self-assurance and confidence, you will never be able to perform and deliver on your success campaign. Most of the time, your mind will revolve around whether you will be able to achieve your success goal or not. The core reason of lack of self-confidence is fear of failure and lack of belief in self. As said earlier, these fears most often are due to your negative thinking, childhood unpleasant memories and unconstructive attitudes. Believing in self is a strong pillar and habit of your mind and you are the architect of this.

Strong belief in self and success go side by side; each is dependent on the other. Leaders in different professions are admired for their self-confidence which makes them stand out tall and be counted. A high level of self-belief is a great motivator, yet many struggle with it and often it retards their growth and moving on to the success squad. Those with lack of self- belief usually fumble when inter acting with people, become nervous, blush, stammer, and carry complexes. When you have a strong self-confidence, you not only inspire confidence around, but book your self on a flight to success. Beliefs are an outcome of your observations, ideas, and thoughts. These change to feelings and ultimately into beliefs and get registered in your subconscious mind. Details of how beliefs are formulated are given in chapter 12. Your beliefs have a powerful affect on your expectations and if you firmly believe you are destined to become successful, then this has a strong effect on your expectations which in turn become very positive. Your success will ultimately be determined by what you believe you are capable of.

After a recent failure or unsatisfactory performance, you may get provoked and for sometime, may lose on self-confidence due to low esteem and lack of optimism. For example, if you feel that a particular task is difficult and out of your reach, your mind will get to work to create actions which support this. On the other hand, if you believe you are going to achieve a task, accordingly the mind will get cues and will work in support. **Mohammed Ali, the greatest boxer of all time was a strong believer in self. His belief that he was the greatest took him to the summit of boxing.**

How often have you noticed that most people avoid commenting firmly when asked whether they would be able to perform a task by a certain time period? The usual replies are-**"will try / can't say / might be able to"** or may be simple **"no I don't think."** This is outcome of their lack of self-belief. There may be very few who might say, **"Yes I will do it."** Most are either unsure or don't want to commit and be in a safe mode. Sometimes, they lack self-conviction and are not sure about their capabilities. Achieving success is no pushover; it is treading through a whole lot of adversities barefooted with **'can-do attitude'** and a well-conceived strategy as your companion. How about concentrating on your success campaign and try to regain motivation and drive by self-talk, i.e. **'No matter what happens I will bounce back.'** Remember, one time confident is usually all time confident. It may be possible that sometimes in spite of confidence, you may not succeed because success is not only confidence but association of many other factors. It shows itself in every aspect of your lives: the way you perceive world around, approach crisis and disaster, the way you treat others, and the way you treat yourself.

Take a look at the following brief true stories of believing is achieving.

- *Former Washington Post CEO, Kathrine Graham, had no idea of self-ability until tragedy struck following her husband's death; Katherine had chosen to fill her husband's shoes as the publisher. Her autobiography, 'Personal History' states that, "What I essentially did was to put one foot in front of the other, shut my eyes, and step off the edge." This bold step and personal conviction led her to become the first female CEO of a Fortune 500 company. Katherine's success can be summed up by her words, "To love what you do and feel that it matters — how could anything be more fun?" 'Personal History' was awarded the Pulitzer Prize for autobiography in 1998.*

- *Ruth Handler, founder of Mattel & Barbie Creator was a great businesswoman from US, is remembered primarily for her role in marketing the Barbie doll. It is said 'that she transformed her belief of girls playing with paper dolls, to dolls with breasts being vital to the child's self-esteem.' That belief led to the icon everyone knows as Barbie. She had a modest beginning and gave dent to her visionary approach by starting her entrepreneurship ability from a garage in 1945. Subsequently, her leadership made Mattel grew to become a Fortune 500 company.*

- *Andrew Stephen Grove, is a Hungarian-born Jewish-American businessman/engineer, author and a science pioneer in the semiconductor industry He escaped from communist-controlled Hungary at the age of 20 and moved to the U.S., where he finished his education. Soon after arriving in New York in 1957, he held a job as a busboy. He later became the CEO of Intel and was a pioneering figure in transforming the company into a giant. Once he told Warren Bennis (a pioneer of the contemporary field of Leadership studies) that "he grew up with a Nobel complex. His parents imbued in him a sense that he would succeed in whatever he attempted. If he went into science, he told me, he felt, he could win the Nobel Prize."*

According to Warren Bennis, "psychological hardiness, the sense that things generally work out well, creates tremendous confidence in oneself and in those around. And that kind of confidence influences others. It builds energy and commitment, and that in turn influences outcomes."

Believing in self does not happen robotically, you need to work for it. The core chestnut of achieving success in life is not due to a supernatural formula, but a strong faith in the self and arousing the potential within and the sermon to act. It is a trust of highest order and on the same footing as your faith in God. This takes place through a command, a drive and keenness which often forces to perform irrespective of impediments. For instance, Zen techniques emphasise development through inner strength, self-discipline, determination and constant practice that helps in empowerment, self-reliance and developing self- power to manage one's goals. This is how samurai (early Japanese warriors) become refined fighters and were able to sense an enemy's attack. The samurai often used Zen technique called 'Za Zen' to concentrate better on the task at hand and to strengthen belief in their ability.

In order to manifest what you want out of your success campaign, your thoughts, emotions and actions must not only be in harmony but synchronize as well. Often most people think about the reasons of not making it. They are usually found drawing on their past experiences and suffer from the self-limiting belief that they just can't do it. Even though their self-limiting beliefs are not based on any facts, yet they always behave in a manner consistent with their unfounded beliefs. **If you believe you can pilot an aircraft, set goals, get trained then you can master all the skills needed in flying an aircraft. Make a decision to adopt beliefs which are consistent with achieving your campaign**. All successful people have beliefs consistent with what they want to achieve.

Often people ask how to retain self-belief when things are going bad and one is under pressure. Well this is the moment when one's self-belief is on test. Irrespective of low feelings and lack of drive, try to be unrelenting, maintain calm, be self-motivated and neutralise negative thoughts by remaining focussed to seek the solutions. Don't forget that, '**courage is the fuel while self is the driver that powers dive and empowerment.**' You can be a 'numero uno' provided you practise strong belief in the self and assume that it is in your DNA. What is needed is a firm resolve, dedication and drive to have a personal experience of **'Believing is Achieving'**.

High on Self-Belief

- ❑ Doing what you believe is right, irrespective of what others say.
- ❑ Taking risks when required. Never say die attitude.
- ❑ Remain positive even during crisis situations.
- ❑ Admitting mistakes and learning from these.
- ❑ Prepared to exert and travel extra miles to achieving your campaign.
- ❑ Self-motivated, persistent and highly passionate to achieve

Low on Self-Belief

- ❑ Unduly concerned about what others say and how they visualise performance.
- ❑ Afraid of failures and underperformance. Avoids risk taking and likes to be in comfort zone.
- ❑ Gets nervous while handling crisis situations. Pessimist and negatively oriented.
- ❑ Lays down arms quickly if there is a problem. Often lacks motivation/desperation and needs repeatedly inspirations to move ahead. Lacks on being self-starter.

> *"You can be anything you want to be,*
> *if only you believe with sufficient conviction*
> *and act in accordance with your conviction;*
> *for whatever the mind can conceive and believe,*
> *the mind can achieve."*
>
> *– Napoleon Hill*

Guidelines to Boost Self-belief and Confidence

Take a look at the following story:-

> *"In a village school, there were two boys, one blind by one eye and the other, most beautiful and handsome. One day one eyed blind's father was carrying lunch for his son to the school. On the way, he met the father of the handsome boy carrying lunch for his son too. The father of the handsome boy requested if he could carry lunch for his boy as well. The father agreed but asked, "How will I locate your son?" "The one who is most handsome in the class is my son." The man went to school, looked around and found his son(one eyed blind) as the most handsome in the class and gave both lunches to his son and left. Later on, when the handsome boy's father asked him as to why he did not deliver lunch to his son? "Well I found my boy most beautiful in the class."*

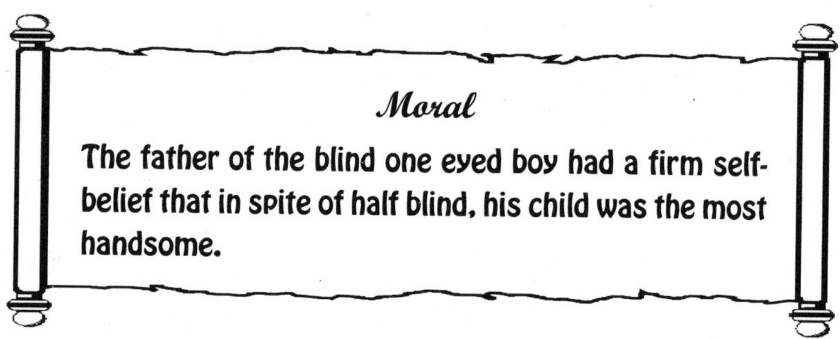

Self-limiting beliefs, such as: less talented, incapable, incompetent and feeling inferior only leads you to settling for far less than what you are capable of. These have to be overcome by self-resolve and will power. No goal in life is achievable unless you train and energise the mind to walk the rugged and uneven road to your goal. Watch athletes in action and often one becomes amazed on their dare devil performances. They have no fear of hurting because they build their confidence levels by sheer self-belief and zeal by working on their subconscious mind. (For details, see chapter 12.)

1. Psychological Make up

As said earlier, your mind plays a pivotal role in building your self-confidence and self-assurance. It encourages you to take the required action to deliver. If you are able to generate optimistic thoughts, it helps to build on your self-confidence. This is possible provided you are able to scan your thoughts from time to time and try to weed out the negativities by positive self-talk and confidence. As said earlier, the major booster of your self-belief is your attitude not by what you can do, but by what you think you can do. As Henry Ford said, **"If you think you can, you can. And if you think you can't, you can't."**

Have a look at the following story:-

A man had a black dog and a white dog and his dog fights attracted large crowds. Every week, people would bet on which dog would win. Sometimes, the black dog won, and sometimes, the white one. One lady noticed that no matter which dog won, the owner would always bet on the right dog and won each time. When the man retired the two dogs, the lady asked him the secret." Simple," said the man. "I always bet on the dog I had been feeding all week."

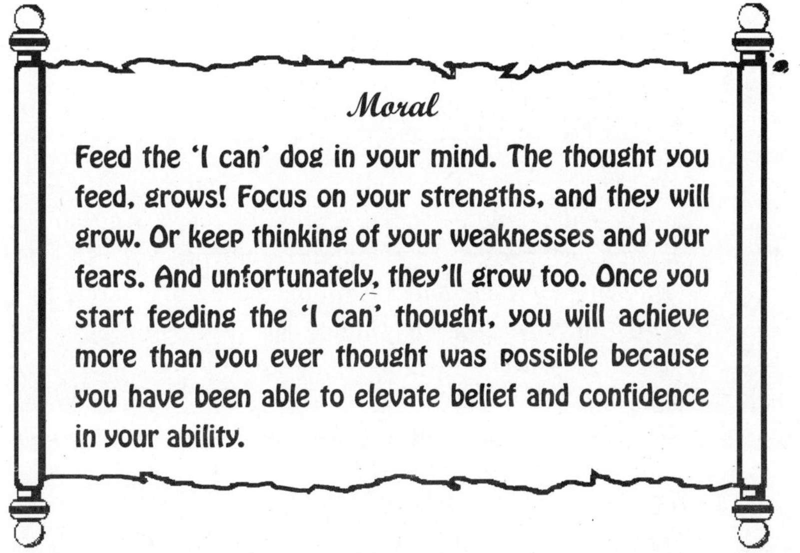

2. Have an Open and Bendable Mind

A flexible and open mind develops self-confidence fast. Start developing it by taking up small challenges both off/on job and try putting your best to complete these successfully. This builds confidence. Next take up in a phased manner, the goal which is a difficult challenge. If there are difficulties in completing or underperformance, don't lose enthusiasm. Rework and not leave it unless you achieve success. It would be advisable to make self-assurance that you are absolutely committed to your campaign and that you will do your best to achieve it. If there are any genuine doubts or apprehensions, these need to be looked at and resolved. Remember, nobody is born with a strong self-belief, we all pick up in our lifetime. Self-belief is not written on the top of the hill. It is there in you and need to be explored. **Re-examine and discard many of the limiting beliefs you have about your self; ideas that you've somehow collected right through your childhood.**

3. Use of Affirmations "Yes, I Can"

Take a look at the following story:-

> *Once upon a time, a family of crows lived on a tree. One day a huge snake came to live in the hole at the bottom of the tree. Soon Mother Crow hatched few eggs and some more baby crows were born. When the crows flew out in search of food, the snake ate up the babies. When the crows returned, they could not find their babies. After a few months, the Mother Crow gave birth to some more baby crows. This time the Mother Crow stayed home when the Father Crow went out in search of food. Ignoring the fact that the Mother Crow was keeping a watchful eye on her babies, the snake still slithered up the tree and attacked the babies. The Mother Crow tried to fight the snake off, but she was not strong enough. Other crows came to her aid, but the snake had already eaten the little ones and crawled back into its hole. When the Father Crow returned, he found all the crows weeping. He consoled his wife who wanted to leave the tree-house*

immediately. The Father Crow said that this tree had been their home for many years and they must live here. He was confident and chanted repeatedly that we will get the snake killed. He thought of asking a wise old fox for help. The old fox came up with a brilliant plan. He told them to go to the river bank, where the ladies of the royal family would be bathing. Their clothes and valuables would be kept on the river bank, while the servants would be watching over them from a distance. The fox asked the crows to pick up a necklace and while away, making a raucous noise. This would make the servants chase them to the tree, where the crows would drop the necklace into the snake's hole. So the next morning, the Mother Crow picked up a pearl necklace and flew off as the Father Crow cawed loudly to attract the servants' attention. The servants ran after the Mother Crow and reached the tree where they saw her drop the necklace into the snake hole. As the servants were trying to take the necklace out with the help of a long stick, the snake came out of the hole and hissed at them menacingly. The servants beat the snake to death. And so, the Mother and the Father Crow lived happily ever after on the tree.

Affirmations are universally powerful and energises your mind to change your beliefs.

Most people are in the habit of starting with negative perceptions about situations, people and events in their lives. Sometimes unconsciously, they repeat negative, gloomy and distrustful statements without realising the harmful affects on their mind-set. As said earlier, affirmations open up your mind to possibilities of altering your views on things and situations that appeared previously out of your understanding and subsequently become relatively easy to handle and change. Affirmations help to change your perceptions and attitudes towards yourself, thinking, feelings and beliefs. With the use of affirmations, you are able to gradually delete the earlier junk feelings and beliefs and replace these with the new 'positive affirmations' to take over and become more focussed. Positive affirmations are like *success mantras* that need to be regularly chanted to tune your mind to achievements and accomplishments. While saying to your self, **"I can do it" or "I will do it,"** you hone your mind's untapped talent and feed it with concentration to achieve the desired outcome, and in the process improve your self-belief. (For details, see chapter 12.)

4. Envisage and Imagine

Visualise and imagine what you desire. Imagine what your life is going to be like once you achieve what you believed in. Initially, it looks just mundane and a joke. But as you go along and repeatedly practise, you will observe slowly that your mind sends command to the body and your total self is focussed on achieving the campaign.

5. Recognise Apprehensions

Carrying apprehensions and anxieties put you in doubt and install fear, and become a real roadblock in elevating your self-confidence. What does the voice at the back of your mind say about your imaginary fears and worries that keep irritating time and again? This could be related to the recent failure or some past regrets. Whatever is making you feel inferior and low in morale, identify it and write it down. Sleep over it in the night and the first thing to do next morning is to tear these off to start feeling positive on those points. Accept that these happened in the past and you have since moved on. It is normal to face doubts and confusion when reworking on your success campaign. List these and spend some time thinking of solutions calmly and rationally. Stretch and think of taking risks that you are confident of managing. Practising positive internal conversations slowly bring in change in your perspectives and are of great help in building your self-drive.

6. Build on Strengths in Personality Dynamics

The general traits required for having a strong self-belief are: confidence, initiative, unrelenting, self-motivation, achievement oriented and self-drive, etc. Think for a moment and evaluate these and if there is need for improvement, go ahead and self-improve. **Remember, how Sylvester Stallone built on his self-belief in film Rocky and turned adversities to his favour. Visualise him to convert weaknesses into strengths.** For example, in organisations, one has to be a self starter and not wait for manager's instructions and constant follow up. Reach out to colleagues and peers to help build self-belief and confidence.

7. Turn Opportunities to Challenges

Opportunities in life are not given, one has to create and convert these into challenges. Managing challenges builds morale and self-confidence and at the same time, you pick up on new skills and experience multifarious activities. Remember, you are the architect and implementer of your self-confidence. There are times when you may get into emergency situations. Don't be a mute spectator, if possible jump in the fray and try resolving the crisis. This increases your self- confidence, gives dent to your initiatives, increases drive and builds on attitude of a real competitor. I always believe that; Act as if it was impossible to fail. **Act as if you were close to a win.**

8. Don't Carry Complexes

Self- effectiveness in managing and performing a task and confidence are foundations to your self-belief. By building on self-effectiveness and optimism, you are able to improve on self-assurance levels that keep you motivated and going irrespective of obstacles. Try making an assessment of the current level of self-effectiveness. Never feel dejected nor carry complexes if at times you underperform, instead make a note of it and rectify. Continue focussing on encouraging thoughts, images and feelings and you will notice change and vigour.

9. Keep Balanced Expectations

Staying with balanced expectations and emotions is of great help. The key to strong self-belief is to understand and accept that just as low self–belief isn't good, similarly an over self-belief may be setting yourself up for a big let down. Try to keep expectations realistic and balanced by reminding the self that every one has limitations. When you make mistakes and slip-ups, don't try to hide, you only harm your success campaign. Remember, what you believe about yourself matters more than what anyone else thinks about you.

10. Build on Exterior Personality

Your way of walking, interpersonal communications, conduct, etiquettes, ambience, and dressing sense speaks volumes about yourself and are a preamble to your being often generating an aura around. Build on these step-by-step and get it audited by a friend or colleague. Your self-confidence can be assessed by others when they make an eye contact with you. People with low self-confidence hate making eye contact. They would tend to look at the ground. The eyes undoubtedly leave an everlasting impression on others. By practising good posture, you'll automatically feel more confident. Stand up straight, keep your head up and make eye contact. You'll make a positive impression on others and instantly feel more alert and empowered. Physical fitness has a huge effect on your self-confidence. If you're out of shape, you'll feel insecure, unattractive and less energetic. By working out, you improve on your physical appearance, energise yourself and accomplish positive manifestations.

11. Build up on Social Skills

Having flair for social skills and interpersonal relations leads to developing of confidence and is also an opportunity to learn from others. Try smiling casually at people that you meet on the street. You will be surprised at how most will throw back a smile at you. Appreciations and encouragements received add to your self-confidence and boldness.

12. Build Power from Within

As said earlier, building power from within is an internal driver and is created by building strong mental images of how you'll feel and experience as you achieve your success campaign. Visualise self-addressing a gathering of several hundred people on how to increase belief in the self. Imagine yourself repeatedly raising hands, performing body acts, asking questions from the audience and using humour to put your thoughts across. Imagine people giving you standing ovation, etc.

13. Keep Self-Motivated Irrespective of Problems

As said earlier, anxiety and demoralisation only retards your motivation and zeal and makes you mentally weak. If your confidence levels remain intact, sooner you will be able to confront the problems head on by evaluating and implementing suitable alternatives provided you remain persistent. Secondly, imagine how you are going to motivate your child if he loses confidence in obtaining better grades in school. The same assurance and moral boosting you have to give to yourself. Initially, it may appear little difficult but as you practise, you will gradually learn to reinforce and reenergise the self. Remember how you learnt bicycling and later on driving the car. Similar motive and drive needs to be initiated. Read motivational literature to develop and broaden your set of beliefs. Remember, great leaders are great readers because they understand the power and influence of books.

CHAPTER 1

Techniques to Build Self-Motivation

Learning to improve belief in your abilities and being confident on your success campaign goes great guns in making you start feeling self-motivated. How about turning your mind to a recent failure or unsatisfactory performance and think whether you were capable of performing much better than what you did? Why your dream of accomplishment remained unfulfilled? Why friends/colleagues/relations have gone ahead of you? How can you rebuild from ground zero to convert failure into success? Why the failures and successful start with the same possible energy, yet somewhere down the line, failure is unable to unleash potential while the successful ride on these? Why sometimes you felt that you were capable of achieving more than others, yet you failed to perform to the best of your capabilities? How did success achievers drove their eagerness to do everything that made them stand apart? The answers to these and similar questions may no doubt trouble you but surely this helps build base for improving on your motivational levels to turn the tables now or never. **Please appreciate that self-motivation is a strong pillar of your success campaign and needs to be looked at in-depth.** There are going to be bumpy rides at times, while pursuing your campaign and what would click and carry you through will depend to a large extent on your motivational levels.

There are no boundaries or limits for the self-motivated; all that they do is to recite the *mantra* of success- **"I am confident. I will make it."** Unfortunately, the story with most failures and average performers is to feel comfortable in living a life of routine; undertake work half-heartedly, lack clear and well-defined goal and purpose. They usually miss on having a well-conceived back up action plan. They are often found short of drive to execute above and beyond. Self-motivation does not take place automatically; one has to have positive thinking, attitude of floating and irrespective of success or failure, work uninterruptedly on their campaign. As Thomas Edison said, **"Many of life's failures are people who did not realise how close they were to success when they gave up."** Self-motivation is like 'everyone must stand on his own legs'. At times, self-motivation is hidden in people till they get an opportunity to exploit it to their advantage. There are also times when the potential remains unutilised and dreams appear far off on the mountain hill? It is a key personality trait that can be developed by stimulus, encouragement, moral boosting, counselling and appreciation. At times, it is also infused by an outside excitement, arousal which often acts as a transforming agent and activates energy levels. Self-drive is a force generated internally that energises and inspires to act irrespective of obstacles and acts as a forte for achievement. Zig Zagler, a reputed American motivational speaker puts it in a lucid manner that, **"People often say that motivation doesn't last. Well, neither does bathing- that's why we recommend it daily."**

Developing self-motivation is a way of life and a habit with success achievers. They are generally backed by a strong and flexible mind which does not allow them to get cowed down by setbacks, obstacles, and other daily nitty-gritty of life. It really depends on how you are able to orient your intellect with positive strokes. The levels and usage varies from people to people. Don't at times you become obsessive; have a push for doing something exceptional, etc. These and similar characteristics are an offshoot of motivation and are directed internally for self-start. It was wonder drug 'self-motivation' and sheer obsession that powered the desire of:

- *Sir Edmund Hillary and Sherpa mountaineer Tenzing Norgay to become the first climbers to reach the summit of Mount Everest in 1953.*
- *Michael Fred Phelps who won 14 career Olympic gold medals in swimming.*
- *Dan Osman, to brave the towering elevations world over without taking any safety measures and for his spine chilling "free-soloing" and "rope jumping." But for self-motivation, this Asian American daredevil would have not been bold enough to set a record for a 1000 feet freefall.*
- *Just the other day, I read a true story of one Mansukhbhai Prajapati from Gujarat who turned a natural tragedy into a springboard of innovation and created the Mitticool refrigerator. Mansukhbhai is a potter by profession. When the Bhuj(Gujrat) earthquake in 2001 flattened his pottery unit, a newspaper published his photo sitting amidst earthen ruins with a title: "Fridge of the poor in pieces." They were earthen pots used for storing water everywhere in India, but the word, fridge caught Mansukhbhai's attention. He embarked on his quest to create a clay refrigerator to fill the aspirations of rural folks who held back their desire to buy a refrigerator out of two compulsions: The refrigerator available in the market was very expensive and its maintenance was high. And, second, the power supply in rural areas is erratic and hence, the investment wouldn't have yielded desired results for the buyer. It took him four years of trial and error to finally arrive at a mix that was good enough to create the final product. (Ref: Yahoo! India Education - 25 January, 2012)*

Self-motivation to these great thrill-seekers, low cost innovators and several others was the singlemost important internal force that activated their fanaticism, pledge and made them reach the summit of their mission in spite of facing intense hardships, failures and setbacks.

One important thing that self-motivators do after each activity is to evaluate their experiences in a positive manner. This gradually builds their initiative, self-esteem and powers them to do still better. They take inspirations from Nature and realise that trees don't grow overnight but incrementally through nurturing and sunlight. Likewise, you try to attune to such continuous initiative without anybody's supervision or push and develop a trait as natural as a tree's characteristic to withstand cyclones and thunderstorms. Take a look:-

> *"Helen Keller did not have the power to hear, talk or see. One day as she sat by her sister in class, the teacher held her hand and made her write on the slate. Helen ran to her mother and wrote her name on her mother's arm just the way the teacher made her do on the slate. Her mother jumped up and that moment started the journey which made Helen know much more than many people having all senses. Helen Keller was the first deaf and blind person to earn a Bachelor's degree in Arts. She was a renowned author, political activist and a lecturer. She was a self-motivator and became a role model to millions."*

I feel sometimes the self-motivated are so high on their motivational energy; they see no reason why they can't have a moonwalk. Their motto is what the famous golfer Gary Player advocates, **"The harder I work, the luckier I get."** They have a strong work ethic and commitment.

Make a note:

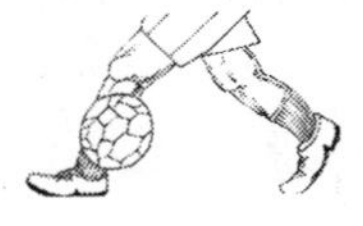

- *Every time you pursue success, imagine football your action, passion, and desperation, while net your goal and mission. Like a footballer dreams putting the ball in the net all the time so do you need to repeatedly visualise accomplishing your success campaign.*
- *Once the self-motivator makes up his mind, everything else falls in line, the energy flows through the mind and the body responds, the goal/target becomes easy to achieve.*
- *Self-motivators have nothing to lose in spite of failure because their greatest achievement lies inside them which*

is like a cell phone charger that charges storage batteries every time they are weak or drained.

- *Motivation can be induced and built provided you have a proper environment of appreciation, encouragement and inducement of enthusiasm.*

My equation for self-motivation is as under:

Self-Motivation = (Positive Mind + Self-Belief + Visualisation + Persistence + Passion) **Minus** (Lack of Self Discipline + Just Running on Own Inertia + Looking For Easy Options + Inconsistency + Fear of Failure + Constant Follow Up) **Multiplied By** (Winning Habit) = **Excellence in Success.**

Guidelines to Become Self-Motivated

1. Remain Encouraged and Enthusiastic

Drive to perform does not sprout in isolation nor does it take place when you are low due to a recent failure. One needs to first stabilise feelings and then uplift the mood by going out or playing with children or even watch a funny and humorous movie or read a book, etc. Once the feelings are totally back on track, plan to gear up and service motivational factors, such as: expectations, fear, hope, doubts, positive emotions and feelings, self-confidence, zeal, enthusiasm, gusto, etc. These are the pillars of self-motivation and strengthening these is essential to come out of the closed shell and perform fearlessly. It is advisable to look for as much support, morale boosting and support from family, friends and colleagues as far as possible.

2. Stay Upbeat Daily

Your mind requires the right environment, be in the top gear like your daily physical exercises to keep your body fit and agile in order for it to function properly. This keeps your motivational levels agile and rearing to perform, otherwise the motivation may lose its drive. Take some time off to read, watch and listen to inspiring and encouraging stuff everyday to remain focussed. Just a few minutes a day can make a huge difference and help you to stay focussed on what's important. Each morning when you get up, focus on some beautiful painting or flowers in your room, even looking at portraits of Gods and Goddesses gives inspirations and positive strokes. Remind the self of your dream of accomplishing the success mission. Visualise how elated you will feel when the campaign is accomplished and your mission completed. Wouldn't it act as a great boost of confidence and energy! Say positive things about how your day is going to be and be optimistic that it's going to be better than yesterday. **I would like to repeat once again that positive feelings act as a roadroller to push your motivation and need daily servicing.**

3. First Attempt Needs to be an Easy Attempt

First movement is always difficult, therefore never ever attempt undertaking major and difficult tasks first. Start off by doing some thing easy like in a school/college examination, you may have attempted and solved easy problems first and then moved on to the difficult ones. Similarly in life, solving day to day problems satisfactorily is a good way to maintain motivation before moving on to undertake success campaign. Never ever get bothered 'if people criticize, hurt you or shout at you.' Remember, **'in every game, it is the audience that makes the most noise through hooting and not the players, they just concentrate on their goals.'**

4. Value Self

Never leave your success campaign half way, instead learn lessons out of a temporary stopover. It is said that only 1% of people actually take action and they succeed. Let you be part of this 1% and not the 99%. Appreciate your own garden of achievements, be honest to feel happy on what all has been achieved so far in life. This self-appreciation helps in uplifting the frame of mind and powers the self-motivation instincts.

5. Be in Tune with Nature

Nature is a great source of inspiration and often uplifts your feelings and gives new perspectives, new thoughts and realisation that 'self- help is the best help.' Look at birds and animals, once they are out of their infancy, they have to fend for themselves and nobody helps them in mitigating their hunger. Watch birds, trees, plants, flowers, cool breeze, the rising sun, etc. Observe children playing, people chatting or walking. Stop by and exchange pleasantries. After a little while, sit in a corner and energise the mind by focussing on the success campaign and how to go about completing it successfully. Don't look to Nature only when it is extremely hot/cold or when it rains!

6. Watch Motivational Movies/ Videos

These fuel passion and melt otherwise semi-frozen emotions. While watching, critically evaluate important dialogues. Make mental notes of salient features; imagine the self as the hero fighting against all odds to succeed in achieving the mission. For example, watch English movies like *Rocky, Rudy,* the *Titans, The Beautiful Mind,* or Hindi movies like *Deewar, Do Beegha Zameen, Guide, Do Aakhen Bara Hath,* etc. These have a central theme on motivation and how tides can be turned to your advantage.

7. Read Motivational Literature

Books and write-ups on motivation will always remain a useful support system and provide ample examples, techniques and experiences of great achievers. Failure, feelings of giving up and hard times are part of life and one loses motivation to restart and perform. It is high time you rejuvenate faith in your abilities and reactivate your confidence. **After all, no one walks a brightly lit road all the time, nor one can avoid dark patches.**

Summing up.....

Motivation is an internal drive of highest order and together with right thinking paradigms, good intensions, self – esteem and confidence completes a task par excellence. How about assessing and identifying what drives you before you turn to the next page of this book? Can you build on this drive and extend its scope and internalise it? Self-motivation is like self-help and being a self-starter and is backed by initiative and self-belief. **Imagine mentally that a couple is out on a date to a restaurant, the person who makes and serves the tea is the true initiator and a self- starter, a base from where self-motivator doesn't look back**. Learn from soldiers in the battlefield, for days together they remain confined to a bunker, yet are nimble and self-motivated to fight till their last breath. Motivation needs to be self generated and you alone can keep that fire in your belly alive. **It is a continuous activity just like brushing your teeth, bathing and putting on the best attire daily.**

Power the Self with Determination and Persistence

Once you are confident and motivated, it becomes easier to get into the determination and perseverance mode and feel upbeat, energetic and optimistic that helps power your will to achieve. Determination is an internally driven push which is powered by enthusiasm and inspiration that acts as a stimulus and gives you potency and guts. It gives strength and grit to remain in reckoning, be focussed and manage obstacles and irritants with a cool head and application of intellect. If there is one wish that you need to grant to your self on your success campaign, it is the power of determination and will to accomplish. If you build on your will power backed by a persistent mind, nothing can stop you nor deter you from following your pursuit and fulfilling your desire for success.

After a recent failure, courage and audacity to rebuild from ground zero is a bold and difficult step you undertake to get back on your success campaign. Failure, no doubt makes your feelings low and dejected but your strong will power incites to unearth success from failure like raw diamonds are chiselled to give these indulgent shapes. You need to be serious and goal oriented, have a destination to reach even if carrying with the campaign seems impossible right in the beginning. Bob Knight, Basketball Hall of Fame Coach says that, **"The will to win is vastly overrated as a means of doing so. What is**

more important is the will to practice and the means to execute."

Have you ever thought why there are few who want to sacrifice their leisure and sleep? Why only some attempt to challenge the challenge of success? Why majority lack the killer instincts and hunger to conquer the challenge? Why few obstacles on the way makes some feel discouraged, pack up and be in the comfort zone? Why some attempt success half-heartedly, miss focus and are not sure about their goals. Well the answer to all these questions lies solely with those who want to quit on the way and be where they are. They lack power of purpose because they have never coaxed their interior nor bothered to watch closely with keenness the success achievers. Success is not always a byproduct of good luck or a matter of destiny. To achieve success, use resolve and strong will to create crops even in an unproductive land. The difference between success and failure is the difference between a strong **'I can do' and a 'strong I can't do'. 'Determination marries the former while it divorces the later'.** Determination calls for calm emotions, a clear-headed approach, unabated commitment and fortitude for achieving the goal. How about learning the art of being persistent before going on the expedition for success? The path at times would appear difficult to tread and need the power of your mind to cross over. Thousands have been through this path before unhurt and bruiseless and you are only following them. No one can engulf outstanding contribution unless he follows his persistence instincts and gusto to excel under severe constraints.

The difference between persistence and determination may seem small on hindsight. But both are mutually comprehensive. I feel if one is determined to achieve an objective, it is persistence that acts as a supporting behavioural tool. What I am trying to highlight is that determination powers being persistent. Determination is like a boxing championship, where the defender is determined to give punches to the opponent sometimes against his wishes. Being determined is neither an outcome of past nor future; it takes place now in the present moment. I strongly believe that, **'the tougher the challenge, the higher the reward'**. Determination, resolution and pushiness are virtues of a fighting mind that helps to create a niche to cross the stumbling blocks. For example, a soldier does not leave his post in spite of fierce enemy attack; he tirelessly fights till the last bullet left. Spanish bullfight is all about persistence. The bull and the trainer are both trained in the art of persistence. Both try to win over the other by sheer unrelenting conduct. Vince Lombardi, Football Hall of Fame Coach cautions, **"You play like you practice**."

Take a look at the following story:-

> *A fisherman lay his fishing net in the river to catch fishes as usual. Three fishes got trapped in the net. The first fish admitted defeat right away, didn't challenge the failure and surrendered to her fate accomplice and went down to the bottom of net without trying to escape. The second fish tried level best to escape by performing several headlong in the net, but failed. The third fish was persistent and went to one corner at the bottom of the fishing net. After observing for few moments, the fish hit upon an idea and started scratching the net with her teeth. After sometime, she was able to create a whole in the fishing net and escaped.*

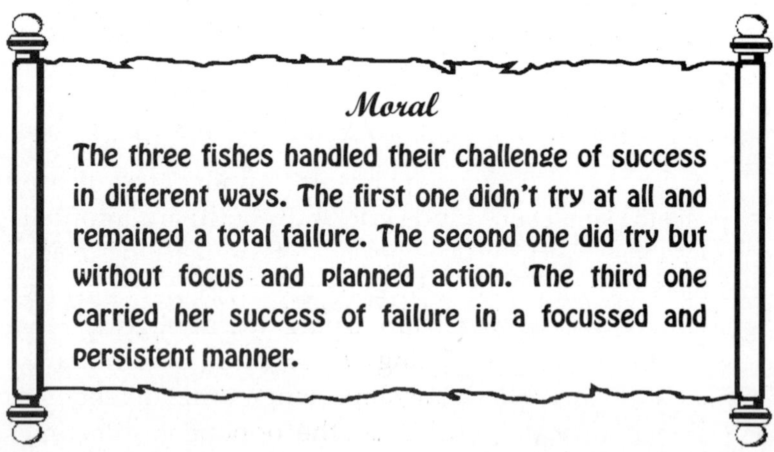

At times on a success campaign, there may be occasions when in spite of strong will power and resolution, yet you may not succeed and feel let down. There is no other alternative other than keep persisting with commitment and dedication and sooner, your success campaign will go for a kill. Some one has rightly said, **"It's never too late to be successful in life, for it's certainly not over until it's over!"** Be a Spanish Armada to conquer success with will power as the commander. For instance, an outstanding footballer depicts his determination right from school/college/national events and finally at international meets. When he is kicking the ball in the world cup final, his mental picture which he had visualised many years back haunts him, activates his power of determination and mind does the rest. His rocket of a header dazzles the opponents. He depicts protégé, shining bright. At times, this becomes his winning hit to bring laurels to his country.

History vouches for hundreds who refused to abandon the ship in spite of facing watertight difficulties and sailing against the current. They were highly determined lot, had a bull's mind that became their surfing boat to garner exceptional success in their pursuits. Their resolution was so powerful that they took failure in their stride. They walked barefooted but didn't compromise with their mission. They were not carrying any supremacy or dominance, but had a pledge with their soul that they will be unstoppable, come what may. They gave command to their self-confidence and physical body to carry on unabated in spite of **persistence wearing resistance**. Many of these strong-willed individuals will be remembered forever for their arduous and gruelling zeal to make a mark for themselves. Some of these great individuals include Colonel Sanders, Charles Schulz, Arnold Schwarzenegger, Christian Keller and an endless list of other great achievers who overcame failures and rejections to achieve their dreams.

In life, anything above routine calls for an extraordinary effort and a spirit to act. Unfortunately, most on a rout not only faux pass, but go several steps back and bend.

They keep shifting focus from one goal to the other, lack self-drive, depict casualness and poor attitudes. There are no readymade techniques to move beyond failure except having unabated commitment and fortitude. **Determination all the way ticks with your talent, tears apart fears and forces you to deliver by a must-not-lose clash with achievement.** Success then is like lighting up the sky on a New Year eve.

All great accomplishments are as a result of extraordinary determination and drive. The construction of Brooklyn Bridge connecting the New York City and Brooklyn is a classical example of strong determination and perseverance with the goal. Take a look:-

- *In 1883, John Roebling, an engineer was inspired by an idea to build a bridge connecting New York with the Long Island. Roebling shared his vision with his son Washington, an upcoming engineer. Working together, they developed the concept. While the project was in its infancy, a tragic accident on the site took the life of John Roebling and Washington was injured and left with a certain amount of brain damage, which resulted in him not being able to walk or talk or even move. In spite of his handicap, Washington continued with his burning desire to complete the bridge. As he lay on his bed in his hospital room, suddenly an idea hit him. All he could do was move one finger and he slowly developed a code of communication with his wife. He touched his wife's arm with that finger, indicating to tell the engineers what to do. For 13 years, Washington tapped out his instructions with his finger on his wife's arm, until the bridge was finally completed. Today the spectacular Brooklyn Bridge stands in all its glory as a tribute to the triumph of one man's indomitable spirit and his determination not to be defeated by circumstances."*

Sujata Burla's life is an example of 'where there is will, there is way'. This is one such example from thousands of a never-say-die attitude that overcomes a terrible physical handicap in achieving an impossible goal.

- *Sujata Burla's life is an example of 'where there is a will and determination there is a way'. Her life was shattered in 2001 when on a pilgrimage to Shirdi, Maharashtra she met with a serious accident, survived but life dealt a cruel blow when the doctors and physiotherapists treating told her, she could not walk for the rest of her life. The accident had turned her into a paraplegic. It meant Sujata was immobile below the shoulders at the early age of 21. Before the accident, she had many friends but they all left her one by one after the accident. While she started feeling alone and depressed, yet another tragedy fell on her when in March 2004, she lost her father. She didn't get cowed down by her circumstances and wanted to be independent financially. She started working with her sister, who was a fashion designer and then started a textile workshop on her own, but the workers took advantage of her physical disability and she lost money. She realised that if she had to succeed in life she would have to do something for which she did not have to depend on anybody. She hit upon the idea of working in the stock market and learnt typing and working on a computer. She spent another year learning the nitty-gritty of stock market operations. This was the turning point in her life. Today she trades like a pro and earns anywhere between Rupees 2,00000 ($4000) and Rs 2,50000($ 5000) every month. It is said that on September 19, 2007, when the Nifty was up 186 points, Sujata made a cool Rupees 600,000($12000) in a single day. Financial independence is what she strove for and she has got it through sheer determination and discipline.*

> *"When you get into a tight place and everything goes against you, till it seems as though you could not hang on a minute longer, never give up then, for that is just the place and time that the tide will turn."*
>
> – **Harriet Beecher Stowe**

Guidelines to Build Determination and Perseverance

Rebuilding from ground zero to convert failure to success does not happen by sheer hard work alone. It happens more out of extreme anxiousness to carry on with eagerness that activates your inner drive. **It is an adrenaline rush, a fury and intense gusto that combines your mind, body and soul to work in unison to articulate the yearning to convert your success campaign into reality**. Determination and being strong-willed can be acquired by becoming mentally tough through self-training, managing failures, facing hardships and by constant practice of not dropping small or big activities, no matter what the knocks are ahead. Before you go further, just think for a moment- **"Am I determined and persistent with my goals or am I an inadequate individual who gives up at the first sign of difficulty or failure?"** Think!

1. Flaming Desire

Do you possess enough fire in your belly for converting your failure to success? Do you keep thinking and craving to achieve your goal all the time? How fanatical and stimulated you are? **Do you possess a strong sensation that creates a push within to rush forward to fire your appetite that powers you to perform even during adversities**? Determination is penchant for appetite and how many of you have developed that appetite to mitigate your starvation for success? Answer to these questions not only motivates and energises you; it also builds a base for your success campaign and helps in sprouting your will. Success, no doubt is directly proportionate to specific parameters of your task that helps in focussing and in turn, builds resolve. For example, it is not sufficient to have a goal of getting a coveted promotion in the job. One needs to be specific in terms of what level one is looking at, the time frame, whether one meets the promotion criteria and what sacrifices one is prepared to undergo, etc.

2. Reinforcing the Self

Steps like encouraging and optimistic self-talk and good inner feelings about your success campaign leads to garnering self-determination and builds enthusiasm. Practising self-control, such as self-discipline and patience to accept delays and letdowns helps in a big way to improve the resilience levels. Problems and disappointments are part of any campaign; do **not fall for easy option of hanging boots and leaving the campaign half way. Look at problems try to resolve these by applying alternative approaches and** keep striving patiently, and success is bound to come. Continue working on the mission without worrying for the results, since the best that you can do is to give your 100%.

3. Practise Becoming Psychologically Tough

Try applying willpower to your daily routine jobs to gain self-confidence and improving on motivational levels. Forget for a moment winning or losing, and instead concentrate on efforts and the direction you need to follow to exploit your inner urge and drive to perform. Learn to meet fear head on by learning and practising managing knots and twists and by being courageous. Physiological toughness means that you should be steady, constructive, focussed and resolute during demanding situations in order to perform at the highest potential, while maintaining a calm head. Be aware of how you will react in unpredictable situations. For example, how would you deal with your subordinates not meeting their job targets or absenting from duty too often. No matter how hard and difficult your campaign becomes, once you are determined to overcome the roadblocks, you will gradually witness the results in an affirmative way. It is also your mental and emotional toughness that is like steel grit that can bear walking hard and real tough extra miles even if it is a path of thorns and thud. When it really gets tough and you are at a handshake distance, it is at this stage that determination fuels endurance instincts to succeed. Staying enthused and stimulated often becomes difficult if results are not coming your way. You need to take inspiration from great people like Soichiro Honda who underwent countless failures, faced innumerable adversities and setbacks for over four decades in search of success. His persistent efforts, dedication and self- belief finally paid off when he succeeded in setting up the Honda Motor Company. (For details, see chapter 14.)

4. Stay Committed

Commitment and determination are mutually inclusive and mitigate your hunger for converting failure to success. When you fail to meet your objective, it is commitment that wills you to go around it and walk right through it. No matter what happens, build and stay committed. What do Sam Palmisano, former Chairman and CEO, IBM, Bob Iger, President and CEO, Walt Disney, Zhang Xin, and Charlene Begley, President and CEO, GE Enterprise Solutions and thousand others have in common? They are all extremely determined and persistent about what they do. Determination to them was like a *mantra* activating commitment to act with fortitude till they became what they are today.

Fuel your willpower by:-

'Sleeping with the goal... Eating with the goal... Drinking with the goal and...Walking with the goal?' No matter what happens, dream successful completion of your success campaign all the time, become anxious like a starved for food or a lover for his beloved. This obsession activates the natural feeling to be firm to walk ahead. In the words of Ralph Waldo Emerson, **"Enthusiasm is one of the most powerful engines of success. Nothing great was ever achieved without enthusiasm."**

5. Resolve is Power that Leads to Success

Depict steadfastness and neverending zeal each day at work – it will be transmittable. There may be days when you may feel low and uninterested. Try to internalise these negative emotions and not depict to others. Power of determination demands to be optimistic, unreserved, cool and smiling irrespective of confrontations and dialogues within. This is the USP of strong-willed leaders in corporate world who inspire employees, strengthen their customer base, build passion in brands and harvest the benefits of their shared teamwork. **Goal, ambition, intense motivation and focus are wheels of success but determination is the fuel that ignites the engine and makes the wheels run up to and beyond success.** A well-planned integration of these five elements brings desired results. But for your determination, all other elements will remain motionless.

6. Learn from Other's Experiences

Find out true success stories and learn from their experiences. Often success stories act as a moral booster and activate obsession and worry to excel. Staying with resolve and grit is like bringing sunshine in your efforts. Take ownership of what you want to achieve and determination will be at your beck and call. Spend time with people who depict strong will power and are anxious about achieving their goals.

7. Be Self-Convinced

'Success is hard nut to crack and being persistent is the nutcracker'. Self-convincing derives from your inner self and means having faith in your strengths and judgement, i.e. able to take risks, meet new challenges, and to deliver on time. In most of the situations, you generally know what the right choice is and more often you are certain about it. Self-convincing is generated by being positive and hopeful that provides momentum and also intimidates you to perform even under unsympathetic conditions. You have to constantly think in confirmatory and be assenting that confidence will garner thrust to your persistence levels. Often most people feel that life is upsetting and why fight back because they predict depressing outcomes. It is through and through your determination levels which acts as a moral booster and gives optimism and confidence to your endeavours.

8. Don't Wait for Things to Happen, Make Things Happen

There is a famous saying that, **'If you can't break the wall by punching it then don't keep punching. Go grab something to break it down with.'** The message from this quote is not to repeat same method again and again but keep trying alternatives to reach the destination in the shortest possible time and with the least resources. Don't wait for outside intervention for things to happen, make things happen by self-action, inventiveness and passion. Never ever melt under stampede of failure. Keep carrying on till failure melts down and you are able to tame success. Don't forget that winning comes at a price, pay through persistence and extreme anxiousness to perform even if success appears mind-boggling and farfetched. Take a look at the following story:

> *"Two frogs fell into a deep cream bowl. One was an optimistic soul. But the other took the gloomy view. "We'll drown," he lamented without much ado, and with a last despairing cry, he flung up his legs and said, "Goodbye." Quote the other frog with a steadfast grin, "I can't get out but I won't give in, I'll just swim around till my strength is spent, then I'll die the more content." Bravely, he swam to work his scheme, and his struggles began to churn the cream. The more he swam, his legs a flutter, the more the cream turned into butter. On top of the butter at last, he stopped, and out of the bowl, he gaily hopped."* (Ref: Month of Inspiration)

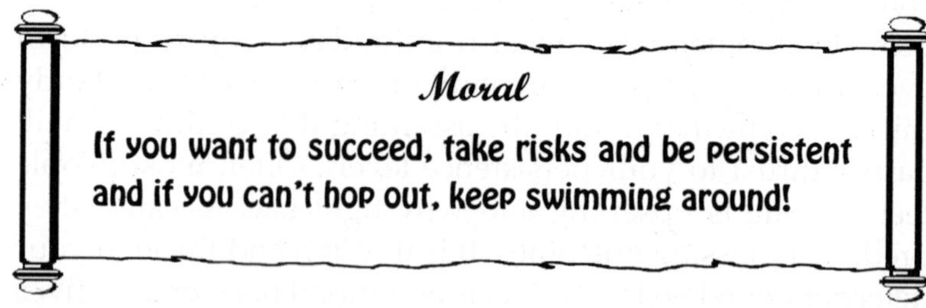

9. Control Temper and Mood Swings

Controlling mood swings and stabilising rage is important. There are times when you are in no mood to continue working, especially if results are not coming forthwith. Any stoppage is only going to loosen grip on the situation and you may be unable to find motivation and anxiousness to perform. Sometimes in life, one has to go against the low feelings and hindrances rather than wait for these to move away from your path. Let you stick to your guns and continue fighting it out; no matter how long it takes. Never ever neither suspend nor look back, just draw attention to accomplishing your success campaign. Remember, the line between success and failure is drawn with a chalk. One strong boost of persistence is all that is needed to push and set on motion your steadfastness that converts self-faith into self-exuberance and the rest will become history.

10. Develop Dedication

It is not possible to be unwavering and steadfast if you lack on dedication which is a foundation of persistence, resolution and commitment. Research shows that when you are internally provoked by self-inspiration to dedication, you will stay put to be persistent. I think it's useful to ask the self, "What level of dedication I have for accomplishing the campaign." "Can I improve first on my dedication and commitment levels? What are the objectives of my campaign and what is my intent?" There are going to be periods in your success campaign, where you will completely lack self- motivational fuel to encourage marching forward. Well it is sheer dedication to your purpose that will decide how long you feel you can continue in spite of non-appearance of results or excessive delays.

Out with the Negative Thinking Patterns

Rewind life to childhood days and realise how your experiences, beliefs and events have left a permanent mark on your thinking patterns. As you grew, little did you realise that these experiences and beliefs will become part of your inner personality and decide your future course of life? On a failure in achieving your success campaign, negative thinking gets habituated in your mind that often leads to affecting your feelings and opinions. A small failure or let down, at times has a snow-balling affect on your intellect by producing unimaginable negative thoughts. It is like a small bushfire leading to a jungle fire mentally. You start blaming your destiny, not realising that you are the driver of your own **'thought chariot'**. Out with the negatives is a process of change and an important step in rebuilding from ground zero on a failure.

Generally, most people are habituated with negative and destructive thinking patterns that result in failures on professional and social fronts and create major hassles in achieving their objectives. Let us admit that each one of us does think unenthusiastic at some point of time. But some of us immediately realise our thoughts and turn our focus away from these. Unconsciously, we take initiative to control our feelings and realise our gullibility. For instance, try paying attention to thoughts and you will be astonished to realise their monoester attributes. Primarily depressing thoughts are an outcome of anger, desire, greed and ego. These get manifested into feelings such as: social comparisons, backbiting, jealousy, dejections, grief, fear, hatred, resentment and hostility, etc. The real problem arises when such thinking patterns get into a auto-pilot mode without your realisation and you start mentally visualising images and thoughts which may or may not be true. For example, if you undertake an assignment at work and fail to complete it in time, you generate automatic thoughts, such as: a) "My boss would be unhappy" b) "I will be fired from my job and I will not get my annual salary raise."

Negative thinking patterns are contagious like swine flu and if not controlled in time, these multiply and wear out your spirit. Those infected by it spend their lives being unhappy, dissatisfied and fail in their intent every now and then. They seem to be surrounded by dark clouds, acidic fumes and cribbing attitudes all the time. They are usually found living a life of disgruntlement and disillusionment. Their minds always appear as if surrounded by a hurricane. They live a life of skepticism and often underperform in whatever they do. *Take a look:-*

> *"Tanzan and Ekido were once travelling together down a muddy road. A heavy rain was still falling. Coming around a bend, they met a lovely girl in a silk kimono and sash, unable to cross the intersection. "Come n, girl," said Tanzan at once. Lifting her in his arms, he carried her over the mud. Ekido did not speak again until that night when they reached a lodging temple. Then he no longer could restrain himself. "We monks don't go near females," he told Tanzan, "especially not young and lovely ones. It is dangerous. Why did you do that?" "I left the girl there," said Tanzan. "Are you still carrying her?"*
>
> *(Ref: inspirationalstories.com)*

Moral

How you become attached to thoughts and carry these for a long time leads to your suffering and adversities.

Most people are always mulling over to have big bank balances, movable and immovable property; high salaried jobs, etc. However, they lack doing hard work and being persistent with their goals? They keep looking for big living rooms in their apartments, but continue with narrow and inflexible points of view. Some of them may be broken inside, have broken families, but fail to reduce their narrow-mindedness, ego and intolerances. Unconstructive people are masters in creating problems rather than solving these and purposefully lend a deaf ear to reaming positives. They would prefer to suffer and suffocate, but not change their thinking patterns. As said earlier, constructive thinking is a habit and a way of life that is either inculcated from childhood or acquired gradually in the later part of life through a beneficial family and school environment, parental guidance and self-faith. A major role is also played by your work/social surroundings, the type of direction you develop for life and also your own *karma*. That is why it is said that, **"Success is the attitude; failure is the lever."** Descartes quote is full of wisdom, inspiration and should always remain a backbone of your thoughts, **"I think, therefore I am."** The quote reminds us that, what we think, we become or get. I have always believed that, **"An upbeat mind is a confident and contented mind."** Acquiring and implementing forward-looking thoughts do require repeated practice, change of orientations towards life. It is true that on a failure remaining positive looks difficult. But at the end of the tunnel, rewards are equally challenging, captivating and self-satisfying.

Just think!

- ❑ Positive thinking supersedes all other personality traits for success. It is a pedestal from where you perform and infuse dynamite to conquer the inner demon, and launch an attack on achieving success.
- ❑ Being constructive may not make you a millionaire overnight nor give success right away, but don't

forget it surely does build a base for ensuing success in the near future.

- ❑ Winners empower their failures as stepping-stones to success by regaling out of setbacks and hard conditions.
- ❑ Being constructive improves your relationships, imbibes happiness, prosperity and inches you closer to achievements.

How negativities generate

As said earlier, negative force springs from the evil part of your mind and may also have one or more of the following reasons:

1. Your senses of perception observe thoughts that may be good, compassionate or devilish in character. In an emotional state, you are neither able to decipher nor avoid these.
2. Usually, when kids misbehave, parents start howling on them, give time out, lock them in a room, install the fear of ghost, etc. Some are accustomed in calling kids stupid, foolish, duffer or statements like "you will not learn," etc. These slowly generate negative feelings among kids and start getting stationed in their subconscious minds and this keeps growing as they grow.
3. Parental relationships that have ended unhappily or unpleasantly may leave a negative impact on the child's evolving mind. There are also times when children observe their parents fighting, carrying out physical abuse on each other, undisciplined behaviour, speaking lie, hiding things, etc.
4. When you grow as adults, past memories of failures; rejection, humiliation, and embarrassment, etc. haunt and remain alive in your subconscious mind and keep generating negative thoughts and attitudes.

Guidelines for Controlling Negative Thoughts

1. Nourish Upbeat Thoughts

It is common to witness most people self-possessive, unconcerned and individualistic. They laugh too little, but get angry too often. They appreciate others rarely, but depreciate them often. They are often envious and jealous of others, but are least considerate and humane. These and similar characteristics picked up over the years have often made some of you downbeat. Rebuilding from ground zero on a failure is an initiative for change and learning a proactive behaviour.

2. Learn Absorbing Upbeat Habits

Replace depressing thoughts to optimistic ones by absorbing constructive thoughts by being persistent with self-beliefs, non-judgemental opinions, caring and sharing, helping people in need, building morale of demotivated ones, changing outlook towards people and situations based on facts and not perceptions and beliefs. Absorbing positive habits is a behavioural change and happens gradually by practice and commitment to change. Learning and absorbing positive habits are must and not necessarily magic medicine to your failure, but surely a step in the right direction and will give dividends as you go on to accomplish your goals.

3. Respect the Feelings of Others

There are occasions when you feel unhappy and frustrated because of bad conduct of people you may be interacting with at work or socially. Your response and reactions to an incident/statement speaks volumes about your feelings. At times, you may be tempted to hit back. These are difficult times, so try maintaining calm and just react by a smile. Don't do an emotional striptease. As said earlier, you have no control on outside circumstances, but surely you can control your reactions to these. Similarly, if someone criticizes, speaks at your back or passes a sarcastic remark, just digest and ignore it. Try to get out of tit for tat as it doesn't pay in the long run.

4. Develop Good Interpersonal Relationship Skills

Have you noticed that conflicts and unhelpful conduct often arises because you look at others from your own perspective and awareness which often may be different than the actual? Quality relationships are an important basis for positive and successful human relationships. Fruitful interaction involves understanding and appreciating individual differences. Much of the interpersonal relationship attributes are largely picked up from your home environment, parents and societal interactions. As you grow, these get developed further or deteriorate depending on your life situations, success/failure and hardships. The dynamics of positive interpersonal skills call for an attitude of sacrifice, broad vision and heartfelt feelings. People driven by head and heart combination generally do well in people management and get accepted quickly. I would say in terms of interpersonal skills, former US President Clinton has positive and par excellence people relationship skills. Can we learn from him?

5. Communicating a Preface to Your Thinking

Your communication style reflects positive or negative feelings. Often unconsciously, you give out positive or negative vibes which are caught by others. It is important to have stable feelings without anger, preconceived notions and ideas, etc. Plan the contents, i.e., what to convey and the mode of delivery in advance. Time and again, you may communicate through body language, i.e., non-verbal clues. At times, unconsciously your body conveys meanings against your intentions. Be careful of body language. Minor conflicts or disagreements at times result in blocking constructive communication, such as stop communicating for days together. This is a sign of immaturity. Don't ever get into a silent mode and block communicating. Give a long pause, say few hours to cool down tempers and bad behaviour before resumption.

6. Elasticity Leads to Positive Performance

Flexibility in your thinking and approach is usually a preamble to a positive behaviour. Take a look at the following helpful tips:-

1. Inflexibility, rigidity and unbothered attitudes are the biggest enemies and are generally offshoots of your thinking patterns. Just think, what is your resolve on these?
2. People with such traits are loner and have problem in relationships. Family or organizational goals necessitate cooperation and help at each stage.
3. Improving way of life requires tolerance, fortitude, firmness and grit. Start from home and make notes each time you are unbendable and think how you could get over this problem.

7. Downbeat Thinking Leads to Disappointments

Constant negative thinking slowly leads to frustration, aggravation, irritation, disappointments and mental trauma that affects your success campaign and derails focus on achieving your mission. For example, if you are repeatedly restless, fretful, feel low and demotivated, you generate fear of failing in your pursuit and consequently underperform. This is due to the reason that thoughts, beliefs, perceptions affect feelings and sentiments. It is therefore important to identify and analyse reasons of feeling low and downbeat. There may be a genuine cause for the same and that need not be put under the carpet but instead resolved on priority.

8. Carry Unbiased Mapping of Thoughts

For a minimum four to five days, try to make notes of whatever thoughts cross your mind including your attention and retention on a notebook. Jot down even if the mind gets attracted to the opposite sex, wants to hit a person, reacts to a comments passed, etc. Jot down if there is a dream in the night and you remember it. At the end of the fifth day, group the thoughts under positive and negative. Try to assess the thoughts and see the path these follow. While mapping thoughts, you will be surprised to know how hundreds of thoughts jog in your mind during the day. Most of these are negative, undesirable, junk and affect your performance.

9. Identify Major Negatives

Lie down on the ground and close your eyes. Now imagine as if you are going to die. Just before dying, you have been granted 15 minutes to think and list the five most important thoughts which you will carry along. Similarly, list five thoughts which you would leave behind. Out of fear and surcharged feelings, you will be honest to yourselves. This way you can try and identify the major negatives and repeat this exercise every alternate day. Request the spouse/sibling to become a partner/auditor in the change process. Request them to maintain a diary for recording the brief contents of negative utterances and thoughts exchanged at home or social gatherings. These can be discussed and analysed on a weekend and corrective measures undertaken in a phased manner.

10. Control Anger and Aggressive Attitudes

Read the following Zen story:

> *A bad tempered boy was given a bag of nails by his father to hammer one in the fence every time he lost temper. The boy took 37 nails to the fence and gradually, the number came down. He discovered it was easier to hold temper than to hammer nails. Finally, when the boy didn't lose temper at all, the father suggested pulling out one nail each day that he was able to hold his temper and the boy did the same. The father said, "Look at the holes in the fence, it will never be the same. When you say things in anger, they leave a scar just like this."*

Just recall the moment you lighted a small string attached to a cracker, it blew with a deafening sound. Often most respond to discontent in a similar way. Anger generally is a manifestation of your failure, disappointment, unhappiness, ego, fear, losing power, injustice, hurt, irritations and struggles, etc. If you are successful in taming these step by step, a major part of devil within you will start getting controlled and reduce gradually. Although it is not easy, one needs to have sufficient practice, openness to change and clarity of objective. Some amounts of anger are natural, but remember it is a negative power that often destabilizes emotions. If not controlled, it may lead to a state of depression and hold back logic and rationality. It also activates passing pain to others. For instance, a manager gets angry on some pretext on his assistant who in turn passes the pain to others in the department.

Find whether your anger is masking emotions, such as fear, sadness, defence, lie, etc.? No sooner you realise this; your anger would come down realising the true reasons. Depending on the situation, you may remove yourselves from the angry situation till you are a little bit calm. Half of your anger goes away. This needs to be done in a peaceful and respectful manner. Similarly, if you don't like a person find what in that person you hate. You would be surprised to learn that often it is you who has problems in understanding others. Work towards stopping emotional driven behaviour. Judge a person/situation in totality and not pick and choose good or bad spots.

11. Ego Leads to Downfall and Destruction

Ego is an important part of your devilish mind and every human being has it although the levels vary from person to person. As you grow in life, the undeterred success, money, political power, beauty, physical superiority and glamour raise your ego levels and overnight it shifts from meagre I, me, and self to the greatest heights. Coming down from here becomes absolutely difficult. It then becomes part of your lifestyle. Certain amount of ego is necessary for your evolution, growth and developing a sense of pride. It is common to call some one egoistic if he is found bragging, "I did this. We did that," etc. But ego has a vast manifestation and lies dormant in your mind showing its ugly face as you grow in life. It manifests through traits such as: - Inflexibility, rigidity, uncompromising, uncaring, arrogance, selfishness, etc. Egoistics always feel they are right. Their ego does not allow them to accept mistakes or tender apologies. At times with advancing age and also due to failures in life, the ego levels may be forced to come down. Controlling ego helps in improving your weaknesses and improves people acceptability. This is best done at the mental level by observing your thoughts and segregating the one's depicting ego. A role play would be useful. Give importance to thoughts and motivations behind your actions and not how others visualise your actions.

12. Don't Get Sadistic Pleasure in Repeating Negative Thoughts

Avoid thinking and repeating thoughts such as: unlucky, bad *karmas*, inferiority complex, jealousy, etc. Such repetitions become impediments in controlling and getting rid of these. If you consciously/subconsciously keep remembering and repeating, you will fail to move on in life. Try to refocus and concentrate on some bright happening in your lives. This will help in not only ignoring, but also getting rid of these unwanted thoughts gradually.

13. Develop and Maintain a Climate of Brotherhood

Building a climate of brotherhood is a slow process. Have a strong resolve and a will to come out of the usual excuse of 'but, because, and if.' Most often, you know your bad approach and habits but your egos create a wall for amend. Developing helpful thoughts does not happen overnight or without a well thought out plan of action, focus and dedication. Your parents are responsible for bringing you in this beautiful world. They would always remain your first Guru and mentor irrespective of your touching the higher stratum of career and success. Touch base with them in spite of occasional differences on certain matters. The modern concept of leaving old parents in lurch as is prevalent in some societies is a bad *karma*. Try to mend fences by travelling a Mile longer. Imagine your state of affair had they left you alone to fend for yourself when you were a child? Providing love, affection and support emotionally and otherwise is an important step to positive orientations in life and to keep getting blessings.

Take a look at the following emotional Zen story:

> *"A farmer got so old that he couldn't work on the fields anymore. So he would spend the day just sitting on the porch. His son, still working in the farm, would look up from time to time and see his father sitting there. "He's of no use any more," the son thought to himself, "he doesn't do anything!" One day the son got so frustrated by this, that he built a wood coffin, dragged it over to the porch, and told his father to get in. Without saying anything, the father climbed inside. After closing the lid, the son dragged the coffin to the edge of the farm, where there was a high cliff. As he approached the drop, he heard a light tapping on the lid from inside the coffin. He opened it up. Still lying there peacefully, the father looked up at his son. "I know you are going to throw me over the cliff, but before you do, may I suggest something?" "What is it?" replied the son. "Throw me over the cliff, if you like," said the father, "but save this good wood coffin. Your children might need to use it."* (Ref: inspirationalstories.com)

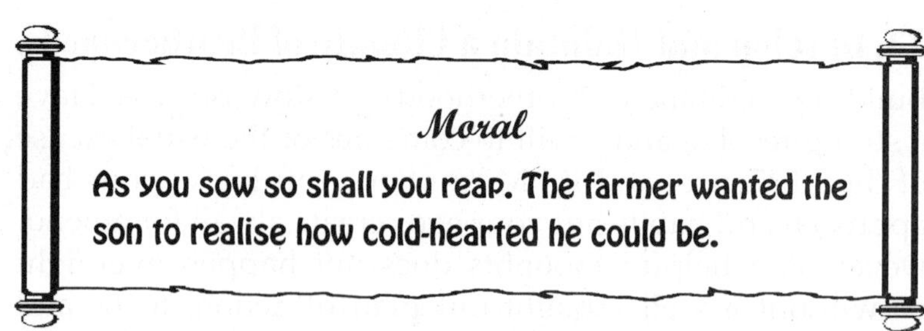

Moral

As you sow so shall you reap. The farmer wanted the son to realise how cold-hearted he could be.

Negative Self-Talk

Your mind is a house to self-talk which is a way of describing all the things you say to yourselves all day long as you confront obstacles, make decisions, observe people, listen to comments and reactions of people and resolve problems. These are continuous and get shaped the way you feel and relate to other people and events as well. Most of it is wiled, imaginative and negative and becomes your basis for action and thus, affects your performance. Constructive internal dialogues on the other hand are an outcome of stable thoughts and feelings and are essential attributes for success. These lead to controlling anxiety levels and activate the desired actions for completion of your success campaign and tend to be useful in proactive behaviour and actions. For example, all scientific enquiries begin by positive self-talk before these come in to the laboratory. Creativity is an offshoot of positive internal dialogue. Constructive self-talk as a cognitive process is often used in sports to build self-motivation, confidence and morale. Controlling self-talk is a difficult proposition since this is a communication with the self and there is no auditor. You remain the conceiver; thinker, responder and usually your analysis are biased and negative. Look at the following example:-

> *Suppose two managers in an organisation are given somewhat identical assignments to manage. The method of attending, planning and action obviously will differ. Manager A may start by saying right, steady and go and launch his attack on the assignment, while manager B may wait, think, evaluate ifs and buts and continue with internal dialogue- "Am I ready? Why we have been given identical assignments? Is there some politics, etc.?"*

In the example, negative self-talk is active in case of manager B, while manager A has already started work and there appears no negative self-talk.

Guidelines to Control Negative Self-Talk

1. Identify Self-Messaging

Control contents of internal dialogue by carrying a self-enquiry analysis:

- ❑ How can I control internally what comes in and goes out? What could I do, right now, to calm myself down? Am I too bothered about what people say or do?
- ❑ I spent too much time in comparing myself with colleagues, relations, friends about their progress in career?
- ❑ How often am I worried or fearful about future? Are my current goals difficult or frustrating? How can I concentrate on my current goal rather than fear results?

2. Internalise Encouraging Thoughts and Feelings

The answer to questions given in step 1 above will help in assessing the reasons that drive self-talk. Take a look:-

> *"I am wasting too much of my mind space in frivolous, unnecessary and uncalled for thoughts. My mind seems heavy and jam-packed with lots of useless past information resulting in all sorts of confusion, conflicts and I am not able to focus on my success campaign. Can I assess what goes on inside my mind and slowly get rid of these by just ignoring and deflecting focussing on these."*

When you internalise encouraging thoughts and feelings and implant these into your subconscious mind through positive affirmations, you take a step forward towards success and proactive behaviour (For details, see chapter 12.)

3. Prune Feelings before Getting Guided by These

Read the following examples:-

1) "I have had consistent good performance during the year. I accomplished all my work objectives and got

appreciation letters from my divisional head. I hope to get rewarded by a promotion this year."

2) "I have tried hard but my luck is not favouring me. My superiors will not promote me. Look there is nepotism and biasness. Yesterday, I wished my divisional head, he did not acknowledge."

The feelings reflected in the second example are negative self-talk. Such feelings often lead to frustrations, anger, de-motivation and are responsible for your disappointment and may ultimately lead to failure.

4. Shift Thinking Patterns, Attitudes and Feelings

Thinking paradigms represent your thought patterns/perceptions about others' situations without knowing the actual facts or reasons of behaving in a particular way. Paradigm shift means changing one way of thinking to another. Going by perception, you are seeing others' situations with a spectacle. Therefore, changing perceptions to the reality helps in changing your attitudes based on perceptions to the reality. By putting your thoughts in the proper perspective you observe that the world around you changes.

Summing up...

Persons habituated to thinking and uttering negative thoughts get branded as negative and it becomes a formidable task to change their brand image. There are no solutions available externally nor blaming others for your plight is of any help. You have to work by being yourselves constructive irrespective of people around. For example, appreciate what you have rather than what you don't. Unconstructive thoughts decrease your self-esteem and can lead to feelings of despondency and discouragement. Just by changing negative thinking paradigms will not pay dividends unless you are consistent with a positive behaviour, such as attitudes, beliefs and feelings and use these in your day to day affairs. At times, keeping an unrelenting positive frame of mind is impractical. This is because of varied and complex nature of day to day problems you undergo and different types of minds you have to interact every now and then. Don't get disconsolate and demoralised when you are surrounded by negative people and situations. Try regaling out diplomatically from the situations if possible.

Frustration, An Unavoidable Part of Success

Frustration is a normal human emotion that often leads to creating mental blocks between you and that of your success campaign. It is a sensation of despair, loss of hope after a letdown or failed pursuit. Frustration is also caused whenever the outcome of your performance is at variance with your expectations and leads to anxiety, anger, lack of stimulus, and despair. Disappointment is your negative reaction to hardships and events that often lead to psychological stress. Because of the nastiness of the feeling of frustration, you will often try and escape issues and concerns that might lead to it. Repeated frustrations reflect your submission to feelings and you are often found thinking internally, "Why the hell is this happening to me? Why others are successful and happy? Am I unlucky? I don't deserve this. It shouldn't have happened to me!" Major frustrations are an outcome of setbacks like: losing a promotion at work, friend in love ditching, spouse threatening to walk out of marriage, health, failure and children not performing up to the mark in studies/profession, etc. Frustrations more often are like headaches which are part of your routine and are all in your mind. No sooner you are able to deprogramme gradually, you witness easing of aggravation. Being able to keep frustrations under somewhat control, allows you to remain happy and optimistic even in the trying times. Robert Bidwell, a professor at the University of Dayton's

School of Business, USA says that 'coping of frustration is best done by being honest, having open communications, fair dealings, and strive to be respected rather than liked.'

> *After a considerably great schoollife, I managed to get on the merit list of a couple of renowned institutes, though not all the colleges of my choice. This frustrated me a lot and I started doubting my abilities and started playing the blame game. The die-hard optimist in me suddenly went missing. Dreams I once cherished became disappointments and the life I once loved became dull and gloomy. For days, I waged a war inside my head and came face to face with my fears and self-doubts. It soon became clear that my fear of failure was holding me back from giving it my all. I decided to face my fear head on and committed to give it my all. Once committed, everything changed. So, today I have no blame game to play, no reasons to look back and nothing to regret. Today, I have some dreams to fulfil, goals to achieve, forts to conquer, roads to walk, battles to win and above all, a life to LIVE and enjoy.* (*Ref: Priya Agarwal, motivateus.com*)

Whenever you are confronted with hardships, frustrations and obstacles, stir yourself with 'I Ching's' great inspiration from the 'Nature':-

> *"When the flowing water...meets with obstacles on its path, a blockage in its journey, it pauses. It increases in volume and strength, filling up in front of the obstacle and eventually spilling past it."*

Guidelines to Manage Frustrations

You have to be aware of the causes that frustrate you. Frustrations will keep coming and going but what is important is to bear with these in the interest of accomplishing your success campaign that has to be on your scanner all the time. What helps is your supportive attitude- **"You have to put more into your life than you take out of it."** Try to lower expectations from time to time when frustration takes over you and instead use your mental energy to your objective. Frustration often is a response to your reaction. Can you try to inculcate the habit of giving a suitable response by finding a suitable solution? The problem has already taken place and what is required is acting on your option based on application of your intellect. This way you may be able to give dent to your feelings. Learn from the frustration and move forward instead of getting worked on it till cows come back home. At times, frustration may act as a motivator to perform better because you have better expectations from yourself. For example, it is always useful to reverse what makes you frustrated and think what you can do to overcome this challenge. This way you are bound to feel in control of your thoughts and feelings.

- Most people often create a benchmark of those whom they are striving to compete and overpower; forgetting that each has a distinct goal, destiny and aspiration, yet they foolishly compare their self-worth. This end ups aggravating their frustrations and disturbs focus and concentration on your success campaign. You need to concentrate on your goal, be patient and reconciliate to tame frustrations.
- Orient the mind to cope with the minor frustrations before launching attack on the major frustrations. This is of immense help in improving the tolerance levels.
- Try to erase from mind your failed attempts and the baggage that goes along with it. Don't resist meeting people neither become paralysed by others' opinions. As said earlier, get back to self-assurance gear; feel secure in social situations by responding with a constructive approach even under pressure.
- Try to distract the mind from the situation that is making you frustrated. Try listening to soothing music or help your spouse in cooking or watering plants.
- Many times, you may be handling problems on the success campaign the same way over and over again and when things don't happen as per your

desire, you often wonder why problems are not getting resolved. Rather than repeating over and over again, can you try to look at alternatives? Sometimes, temporarily letting go the problem helps in controlling frustrations and also gives you time to come up with some creative ideas.

- Frustrations can be real or imaginary depending upon how you visualise an outcome of a setback. Some react by self-pity and become emotionally charged in a negative sense as if the world has come to an end. There are others who on a drop of a hat crib and give dent to their feelings by cursing themselves, their organisation or family. Control feelings and get out from the habit of discussing repeatedly your own problems and the progress of others. People usually give a deaf ear. Try to keep your frustrations to yourself.
- Understand that life doesn't move always according to your choice and will. Frustrations are a normal part of life and will appear and disappear from time to time and you have to live with it. However, your success campaign will get shattered, if you wield under the pressure of frustrations every now and then. Try to learn living with irritation.
- Some amount of frustration can be managed by going on a jog, brisk walk, exercise, taking periodical breaks from work, etc. For example, 'A Brazilian artist opened an exhibition of punching bags in the Santa Cecilia subway station so that commuters could better relieve their frustrations.' Secondly, by regularly maintaining silence and meditating during morning hours helps release frustrations mentally and calm your jumping emotions, behaviours and destressing your mind.

Making Right Choices – The Foreword to Success

On your success campaign, you have to choose often from options available. It is quite normal to feel disgusted on a letdown because possibly the choice you took for decision making did not work. Often at such or similar setbacks, your mind gets worn-out and you wish if some one else decides on the suitable choice and manage this on your behalf. Life is full of hard choices and the more options you have, the more complicating it becomes to choose. Research shows that most people will not choose at all when presented with several equally good options. Making the right choice is an outcome of your judgement, practice, picking up the pedals of right decision making in life and an outcome of flexible and open mind. Before launching on your desired choice, ask questions: Am I on the right track? What are my alternatives? What corrections and change I need to incorporate to achieve my success campaign? As said earlier, how about carrying a total review of your earlier mistakes?

Making a choice whether for small or big goal will always remain difficult and hardest since there is no choice or decision which is perfect. Life is dynamic so are your choices that keep changing with your goals. Sometimes, in spite of making the right moves, yet you may underperform. But this should not stop you from having a relook and analyse what was the cause of letdown and what changes you need to make so that the next time your chosen choice brings in the desired results. The core premise is that **life is like playing a game of cards. Depending on the set of your cards, you have to make the right moves**. There may be times on your success campaign when you may get bogged down and hold back because deep inside your mind psyche you may have strong beliefs that you are a victim of your circumstances and therefore, you are underperforming. But remember, we all go through circumstances of different types, impediments, obstacles, etc from time to time. It's all about how you deal with your circumstances and how you will bounce back hard. Life is all about choices and managing your circumstances by making things possible. Remember, **'if you can't change the circumstances, change yourself.'**

There is no readymade formula to judge whether the choice you have decided is going to deliver to your expectations. Just use your head and heart and remain optimistic all through. Sometimes, you click by trial and error, while on other occasions, it may not work. Don't set hurdles by bothering too much about whether this choice is right or that one is going to click. Just concentrate on your campaign and handle problems as they come. Alexandra Stoddard writes in her book "Making Choices": "You have to be really tough-minded to make choices. The great mystery about choice is that because you will never be able to please everyone, nor even be understood by them, the only hope is for you to feel content about what you decide to do." Therefore, do what you believe is right by taking help of guidelines given hereunder. Eliminate unnecessary things and obligations and find time for yourself. Famous motivational speaker Less Brown in his book, "It's Not Over Until You Win" says, "Learn from your failures and don't allow them to discourage you. Failure is not final. It is not real unless you make it real. The only reality is how you respond to it, whether it makes you better or bitter." Following couplet of Mary Engelbreit is worth understanding and remembering.

Perhaps ...

As you travel through life there are always those times
when decisions just have to be made
when the choices are hard and solutions seem scarce
and the rain seems to soak your parade!
There are some situations where all you can do
is to simply let go and move on,
gather courage together and choose a direction
that carries you toward a new dawn.
So pack up your troubles and take a step forward.

"When someone asked Jerry, a manager of a restaurant how he was doing, "If I were any better, I would be twins!" Many of the waiters at his restaurant quit their jobs when he changed jobs; they would follow him around from restaurant to restaurant. The reason was his good attitude and being a natural motivator. If an employee was having a bad day, Jerry was always there, telling the employee how to look on the positive side of the situation. Seeing this style really made me curious, so one day I went up to Jerry and asked him, "I don't get it! No one can be a positive person all of the time. How do you do it?" Jerry replied, "Each morning I wake up and say to myself, I have two choices today. I can choose to be in a good mood or in a bad mood. I always choose to be in a good mood. Each time something bad happens, I can choose to be a victim or learn from it. I always choose to learn from it. Every time someone comes to me complaining, I can choose to accept their complaining or I can point out the positive side of life. I always choose the positive side of life." "But it's not always that easy," I protested. "Yes, it is," Jerry said, ***"Life is all about choices. When you cut away all the junk, every situation is a choice. You choose how you react to situations. You choose how people will affect your mood. You choose to be in a good mood or bad mood. It's your choice how you live your life."*** *(Excerpts: viewonbuddhism.org)*

Moral

When making choices, you may get attracted to the immediate gains and fail to look from a long-term perspective.

Often the type of life journey you undertake is full of happy moments and sad moments, smooth walks and rough walk. How you handle the rough patches is absolutely your choice out of the available options at a particular point of time. Although there are other elements, such as state of affairs, opportunities, and luck, etc. which play an equally important role, Zig Ziglar, puts it beautifully, **"You are free to choose, but the choices you make today will determine what you will have, be and do in the tomorrow of your life.."** Choice is a command, a mind game that you use each moment of your life when making decisions. Choices will always remain challenging and demanding, more so in case of a failure. Why not take a pause at this juncture and think about some major choices you may have to take to see that you accomplish your success campaign?

> *"An elderly carpenter was ready to retire. He told his employer-contractor of his plans to leave the house-building business to live a happy life. The contractor was sorry to see his good worker go and asked if he could build just one more house as a personal favour. The carpenter said yes, but over time his heart was not in his work. He resorted to shoddy workmanship and used inferior materials. It was an unfortunate way to end a dedicated career. When the carpenter finished his work, his employer came to inspect the house. Then he handed the front-door key to the carpenter and said, "This is your house... my gift to you." The carpenter was shocked! What a shame! If I had known I was building my own house, I would have done it all so differently."*

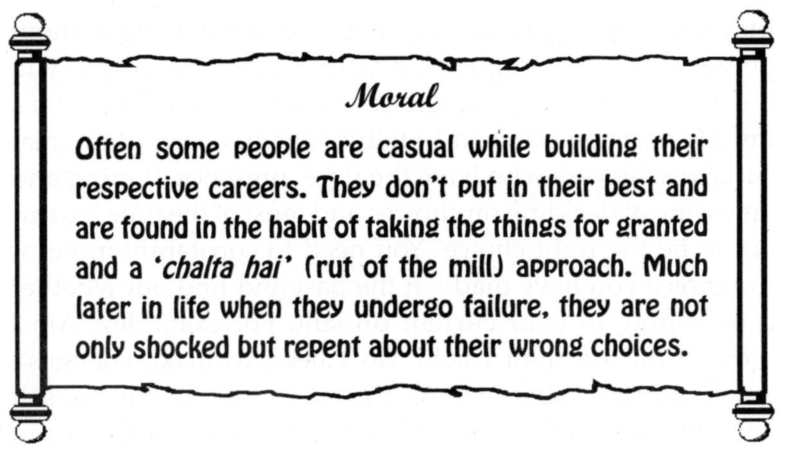

Guidelines for Making Right Choices

1. Improve on conviction, feelings and thoughts

Making a bad choice in life is an outcome of lack of analytical ability and not being judicious enough to evaluate the different available options, etc. When you are in this mental state, it affects your decision making and under pressure of frustration, you may tend to become subjective. Try to incorporate objectivity as far as possible, while taking decisions. Take a conscious choice by never acting on impulses such as: out of revenge, negative attitudes, gut feel, spur of the moment and hunch. Avoid getting swayed by copying others or their suggestions unless making evaluations for pros and cons. Sometimes not being completely clear on what outcome you expect from a situation or deciding for a particular choice calls for extensive application of your intellect and past experience if any. Think objectively what is that you are expecting? Be clear, before deciding on a particular choice by evaluating its effect in the short term and long term on your success campaign.

2. Weigh up the alternatives before deciding

Most people are always on the run to meet and convert their desires to realities. In both meeting their desires and actions thereof, they have to make choices and more often than not, they get tempted to speed up their decision making without giving much of thoughts. On your success campaign, you are duty-bound to think, reflect and understand that even a minute decision can lead to failure again. Learn from great success achievers who have the urge, presence of mind and are aware of deciding on choices and most of the time it turns out to be the right choice. You need to constantly monitor the choice you have made in the past and find out whether it is helping in your current pursuit. For example, "Am I moving on the right track? Do I need to make changes/ amendments? What actions I need to take to put myself back in the driving seat? What are the likely outcomes of *not* choosing this one? What would be the outcome of doing the exact opposite, etc.?"

Each situation in life is unique and so are the choices. Don't change your choice midway unless there is a major obstacle/problem. There may be times when you don't have too many choices to choose from. Select the one which appears best in the prevailing circumstances. Wait for the result, if it is not working. Don't ever get stuck up, just move on. You can also simply write down every option you have for the decision you're making, get it out of your head and spend some quality time on each one.

3. The five ways

Five ways is a problem-solving technique invented by Sakichi Toyoda, the founder of Toyota. He says that when something goes wrong, you ask "why?" five times. By asking why something failed, over and over, you eventually get to the root cause. It was initially developed as a problem-solving technique, but over the years, people have been using it to determine whether a choice they're considering is in line with their core values. For instance: Why should I review my goals? I have had no problems so far. Why is that important? Because you want to accomplish your success campaign and not just the goals are fine and not just have a string of meaningless goals.

4. Take consultations from friends, family and colleagues

Don't allow others to make decisions on your behalf. When you make the decision, even if it turns out to be a wrong choice, yet you have the satisfaction of making the decision and learning from its failure. You'll know you did your best and will have gained valuable experience. Also your satisfaction with your decision will largely depend on whether you claim ownership of your choice.

Get out of being lonely when deciding choices on important activities. Remember, a large part of personal success is based on networking with others to achieve your success campaign. So go out and find "how can I help myself and get benefited from others' experiences?" You may take inputs from friends but the final call on decision and its accountability rests with you. Find out success achievers and champions around you and try learning from their experiences, and be wise.

5. Decide your choice based on thinking, feelings, wisdom and mental picture

It is very rarely that all the ingredients given above will be in agreement, yet it is advisable to go through the motion. Every decision you take has two sides – advantages and disadvantages, but recognise that you are supposed to take an overall view before selecting the appropriate choice. Remember if the choice made turns out to be successful, every one including spouse/ friends/colleagues, etc. will take credit. In the unfortunate event, if the choice leads to a failure, the same people will distance themselves and say for example, "Didn't we tell you? See what happened. You think yourself intelligent and don't listen." This is how most minds work and one needs to listen tolerantly and continue working on the campaign. Never regret a choice that was made in the past and appears a wrong decision today. The circumstances have changed with the time. By all means you need to learn from your mistakes and never make the same again, and move on in life.

Making Right Judgements

Judgement is a key skill that helps to arrive at a suitable decision based on the available information and facts. Making judgement is a part of everyday life and involves thorough studying of pros and cons, analysis of the situation or problem before deciding on the course of action. Errors in judgement are a way of life. But you can always try and be impartial even if it means having a look at your thinking patterns. This assumes significance in case of a failure or performing below expectations when you carry an evaluation to know what went wrong. At times, if your judgement goes wrong and contributes to failure, it not only makes you low psychologically, but also becomes detrimental in reworking on the task. Judgement is a key personality trait that needs usage with utmost thinking to avoid wrong decision making. Take a look:-

> *"A man had a mongoose and his wife did not like it. One day they left the mongoose with their child and went to the market. His wife returned first. She saw the mongoose having a bloody mouth and blood in its paws at the entrance. Worried and angry, she took a big stick and hit the mongoose. The mongoose died instantly. When she entered inside, she saw the child lying on the floor and playing. She also saw a snake bitten to pieces. She realised her mistake. Their mistaken judgement made them lose their pet."*

Judgement Boosters

Get rid of pre-judging habit by practice. It is advisable to read situations' thoroughly, evaluate alternatives, analyse facts, and if need be, go by conviction before basing your choice on your judgement.

1. Don't apply judgement based on your past experiences of success or failure.

2. Every situation is different and changes with time/people/environment/social settings. Understand that what was applicable yesterday may not work today.
3. Judgements need to be impartial and based on facts.
4. Humans are by nature biased. Your preferences come into play which may or may not be right. Try to be impartial for better results. A good judgement calls for clarity of thought and balanced sentiments. Exclude elements, such as: desires, hunches and wishes to keep your judgement impartial as far as possible.

Summing up ....

Each choice you make may result in success or failure or some success and some failure and majority belong to this category. Those who take life choices in their stride are the happiest ones. There are three important phases in our lives – Birth...Living...Death. We have no control on our birth and death. But surely, we have control on our living by our choice and will. Sometimes, the choice we make does not work while at other times, the choice we made worked. We have been through success and failure right through our infant stage.

Be Desperate when Things Don't Go Right

Success comes from aspiration, inspiration desperation and perspiration. Wilting under pressure and quitting may at times, look an easy option but the real hero is one who refuses to bend, stands erect and marches ahead to his desired goal. This is how you change winter to spring in your lives. Life is a 'bet and test' and sometimes, chances of success and failure end up like a probability. Remember, if celebrities and famous personalities had allowed annoyance to take a centrestage in their lives, they would have never reached the pinnacle of their success. Imagine the pressures great Abraham Lincoln would have undergone by facing 29 years of repeated failures, agony and adversities.

I have yet to meet any one who hasn't felt pressure little or big on: failure, success, meeting deadlines, increasing productivity, relationships, health, etc. Aren't you therefore programmed to deal with pressures? When the path of success appears leading to an utter dead end, reverses lead to pain, restlessness and impatience. It is pressure that becomes a stimulating force to make you desperate to perform irrespective of whether the circumstances are favourable or not.

What then is desperation? Desperation is an emotion that arises when you become extreme restless to perform. It also signifies the intense fire in your belly that becomes the hallmark of your achievements. Desperation is similar to the mental state of a non-swimmer when he is thrown suddenly in a swimming pool. He can go down but he gets desperate for his life and in this process, he starts becoming persistent to remain floating by moving his hands and legs. A man once asked, Socrates the secret to success. Socrates took him to a river and asked him to get into the river. When the water got up to his neck, Socrates ducked him into the water. The man struggled to get out, but Socrates was strong and kept him there until the man started turning blue. He pulled his head out of the water and the first thing the man did was to gasp and take a deep breath of air. Socrates asked, 'What did you want the most when you were there?" The man replied, "Air." Socrates said, **"That is the secret to success. When you want success as badly as you wanted the air, then you will get it. There is no other secret."** It was sheer desperation apart from other qualities that was helpful in driving Larry Ellison, the founder and CEO of Oracle and one of the richest men in the world. Lee Trevino puts it beautifully that, **"In the game of life it's a good idea to have a few early losses, which relives us of the pressure of trying to maintain an undefeated season."** Desperation is a driving force that calls for taking risks, being fearless to over come adversity.

The following brief story of a teenaged girl in an air crash is a testimony of how being desperate helped her to survive and reunite with her father. Take a look:

> *Of the 93 passengers and crew on board LANSA flight 508 on December 24 1971, only a 17-year-old Juliane koepcke survived. The plane was struck by lighting above the Peruvian rainforest and Juliane was blown out of the plane, still strapped to her seat, and landed two miles down in the dense thicket. She came round, blind in one eye, with a broken collarbone and cuts and bruises. Remembering her father's advice that where there's water there's civilization, Juliane wearing a mini skirt and sandals trekked for nine days until she found a small cabin. She cleaned her injuries and worm-infested cuts and waited until the occupant came back. She was eventually reunited with her father.*

As said in the earlier chapters, what separate the failures from the successful are their constant hard work, self-reliance and tirelessly keeping head above the water? Success is your willingness to put in extra and stick through frustrating times, and remain floating in the water. At times, obstructions and hindrances become your torchbearer and help you to acclimatise to perform better in stringent situations and conditions that you realise later on when the mission is completed- "My God what all I went through." I always believe that, 'Pressures on a failure is like a shadow and follows us all through; sometimes it hides and walks slowly, while at other times, it increases its speed and necessitates keeping efforts in line with it. Don't forget that 'courage only comes after you have faced fear of pressure and managed it well.'

When rebuilding from ground zero to convert failure to success, inspiration, motivation and desperation become vital organs of your success campaign. Inspiration is an idea that strive you to achieve something of par excellence. While desperation strives to get out of something that really is ticklish, mind-boggling and bothersome. But for desperation, your inspiration and motivation will remain on paper only. Never ever associate desperation with the negative feelings instead use it as a tool that surely digs out your full potential. No doubt enthusiasm is an important companion on the success campaign and energises your drive to perform, but desperation is few notches ahead, it forces you to break the mental chain and pierces through the walls of denial that have unfortunately got built up around your self since all other efforts haven't brought any result. Desperation at times makes you act like a bravado and puts extreme passion to perform. It is a success torch that calls for having resilience and perseverance of the highest order. Richard Branson, the founder of Virgin had his entire career driven by a self-created desperation. He would take loan from the bank for a striving new business and then get in to deep debt and use that do-or-die desperation to take an even more ambitious gamble to pay off the loan. He would repeat with something even more ambitious. Apparently, he was desperate to prove himself and extremely anxious to become successful. **Desperation at**

times is probably a more powerful motivator to make things move in the right and successful direction. When there are extreme desperation levels, you take risks and overcome fear of failure and march to your destination. The story of Wilma Rudolf, who got three gold medals in Athletics in 1960 Olympics is a sheer example of her desperation to success in spite of pneumonia and stroke at the age of four and other physical disabilities and shortcomings which followed.

Desperation often tears apart your shortcomings and becomes your salvo to carry your success campaign through by making use of ammunition, such as hard slog, pledge and devotion. Resort to frantic measures and lead from the front backed by fearlessness whenever success appears withering away.

For example,

> *"On the starting line of the 10,000m final at the 1964 Tokyo Olympic Games, U.S. Marine Corps lieutenant Billy Mills fellow competitors didn't expect him to run a decent race and finish in the middle. A medal for Mills was just a dream. But he stunned the running world. In one of the most amazing moments in Olympic history, this underdog ran nearly a minute faster than he had ever previously run a 10,000-meter race. In the last lap of the race, Billy managed to stay with the leaders, but became boxed in and was then ultimately dropped in the final stretch. Undeterred, Billy went wide and put on one of the strongest finishing kicks in Olympic history—to break the tape first and win the gold. It was the first and only Olympic 10,000 m gold medal ever won by an American. Before this magical moment in Tokyo, Billy had been living a very difficult life. Orphaned at the age of 12, he struggled as he grew up.*

Guidelines to use Desperation

Desperation is converting that intense inner drive, force and passion to perform and be successful. It doesn't happen automatically, one has to carry out a huge mental shake, put all energies to get seriously thinking about what and how to proceed forward.

1. Pressure drives performance

There are times on your success campaign when it becomes necessary to apply self-pressure to reinspire and re-energise yourself. Since it is taxing and requires all out efforts to accomplish a task, some stop short of taking action; and instead are found spending more time thinking about what they need to do. Working under pressure no doubt stretches you, but often it breaks through the limits you've set for yourself. Bear in mind that pressure can help you speed up your efforts subject to its proper application and handling. Focus on solution to a particular snag faced on the campaign rather than the snag itself. Acknowledge the problem and then move on.

Pressure teaches flexibility of bending, not breaking and keep walking to the destination. Pressure is a forceful energy that pushes you and is entirely your choice whether to convert it to a negative energy and get entangled in apprehensions and distress or use it constructively as a self-motivational force to achieve success. There's also a delicate relationship between pressure and your performance. When you experience the right amount of pressure, you try hard to put in your best. However, if there's too much or too little pressure, then performance can suffer. The amount of pressure is directly proportionate to your response, grit and courage. Don't get bogged down with small concerns or work hassles. These are routine and inevitable. Aren't you paid to handle these? The higher the work pressures, the higher the compensation and better the career. Your inner personality dynamics plays a leading role in performing under pressure. If you are outgoing or extrovert type, chances are that you would perform better than those who are introverts and feel comfortable in performing under normal pressure. What type of mind-set and psychological response you have developed over the years makes all the difference.

2. Nervousness characteristics

Nervousness normally arises from negative energy within you that affects your judgement and is in response to external events. The pressure generated by due to this is negative and only results in sliding down your performance. On the contrary if your self-talk is encouraging, the nervousness levels are at the bottom and this helps you to perform better. Also if you are self-confident, you are more likely to perform better under pressure. This is because the aura generated by self-talk and your confidence helps to concentrate fully on the task at hand.

3. Become emotionally rugged

Unless your feelings and thoughts are in a stable condition, these will affect and interfere with your anxiousness to perform. How about developing self-thrill to perform under crisis by walking few extra miles hungry and barefooted?

4. Desperation is a stimulus that drives action

There are times on your success campaign when you may scratch your head in bewilderment, feel panicky and start showing feelings of hopelessness. But fighting battles can't be left half way? There appears ravine both in front as also at the back. Opportunity doesn't wait and you need to rise above the situation to get out of wilderness and use all resources at your command. Move forward, untie knots by tightening the lose ends and cutting across all barriers by being courageous and keep trying different routes. Desperation is a tool that helps realise and correct self-defeating attitudes that empowers to move forward. Understand that desperation to succeed is like searching for *Nirvana*. Desperation and motivation work in unison and put you back on your toes and allow you to get that momentum moving. Desperation is an outcome of high levels of enthusiasm and perseverance and not many are able to generate these attributes within unless they pull up their spirit and improve on their sustaining power.

CHAPTER 25

Patience – A Boon when Going Gets Tough

Arnold Glasgow, an American humorist once said that, **"The key to everything is patience. You get the chicken by hatching the egg, not by smashing it open."** On your success campaign, **patience is going to be your friend, philosopher and guide**. It is natural to feel dejected and angry and impatient when you become conscious that in spite of all the hard work and dedication, yet you were not successful. But remember, impatience cannot fly you to success aerodrome; in fact, it may retard whatever you have achieved. Therefore, understand that patience is your friend in adversity while intolerance your enemy. There are several examples of impatient people becoming patient on a failure, (I being one of them) and this became their flight to success. Remember, **"For every minute you are angry, you lose 60 seconds of happiness."** For instance, just before leaving for your office, you ask your son to take the car to the nearest petrol pump to fill the gas and get the tire pressures checked and return within ten minutes as you have to leave for office urgently. You keep waiting and your son returns after half an hour and you are extremely late for a meeting with your CEO. You get terribly tensed and shout at your son. Your body starts trembling with anger and you start sweating. This is being impatient!

Are you willing to be patient for what you were dreaming and working so hard for? The answer in most cases would be "No." Your mind becomes jaded and worn-out and is filled with senseless chatter and negative self-talk. It is at such tense times that patience becomes the most trusted companion that gives courage and strength to accept delay, annoyance or suffering without complaining. Patience resides in a righteous and stable mind that is able to bear sufferings and struggles during distress and failures. When you are patient you are centred and balanced in your mind and body. However, when impatient, you start physically shaking because of the unbalanced energy that triggers anger and worry. This often motivates you negatively to respond and you end up making wrong choices and actions that interfere with your success campaign. Living in the moment is an outcome of patience. By removing the apprehensions of future and accepting that situations can change any moment, patience remains your only **'knight in shining armour'**. It is one asset that allows being calm no matter what the situations are. It helps to maintain a good balance between the mind and the heart, aids in effective relationships, decision making, leadership and a conduit facilitating happy life and a successful career.

Take a look at the following story:-

> *Archie ate apples each day when he went out to play, but the part in the middle, he just threw away. Then one day as he ate an apple to the core, he caught sight of a seed, wondering what it was for. "If I planted a seed, it just might grow a tree." So he planted the seed in a hole and had faith it would grow, even though it was small. With a shovel he covered the hole with a mound and watered it each day. Every day, he returned with the hope he would see a small sign of new growth from the seed to a tree. But the sign did not come and as time drifted by, Archie started to doubt whether he should still try. "Was an apple tree really worth all of the grief?" As he was ready to quit, he went to his father to ask what to do, and his father told him,* ***"sometimes things don't go the way that we plan. Sometimes people give up when they don't think they can. But to those who keep trying, when no one else will, there are dreams to achieve and great hopes to fulfill."*** *The words struck Archie's*

mind and he would try to be patient and keep trying too. He came every day without fail to the seed and watered it. Then one day, Archie saw the small leaf and a tear filled his eye. It was patience that brought this new life from the ground. He had not given up when the outlook was grim and the tree brought him apples, in times that were sweet. *(Excerptes:familyfunshop.com)*

Patience is like building trust and cannot happen within days or months. It requires sustained efforts, practising calm emotions and restraint. It's like learning to solve mathematical puzzles or regular work outs for an athlete to make a mark that needs endurance and a regular followup. When a good batsman hits an unclean shot and survives getting out, he takes a deep breath and settles in before playing the next ball. Any repetition without calming emotions may get him out. On the contrary, some of you become repeatedly angry and this leads to increased stress, anxiety and impatience. When you are patient, you are able to see the bigger picture and can assess any situation by weighing up the pros and cons which later will avoid major mistakes. Managing impatience requires self-control. By being patient, you are able to understand yourself and others. There is much learning in French writer A D Pere's statement that, **"All human wisdom is summed up in two words-wait and hope."** Take a look:-

There was a monk who was very impatient, the more he tried, the more impatient he became. So he decided that he must get away altogether, to learn to be patient and built a little home deep in the woods, far away from civilization. Years later, a man was travelling in those woods and met him. He was amazed to find anyone living so far away from the rest of the world, so he asked the monk why he was there all by himself. The monk said that he was there to learn to be patient. The traveller asked how long he had been there, and the monk replied, "seven years." Stunned, the traveller asked, "If there is no one around to bother you, how will you know when you are patient?" Annoyed, the monk replied, "Get away from me; I have no time for you."

Moral

Whenever you get impatient with your quest, you need to imagine the monk and control your monkey emotions.

Patience in corporate settings aids in team management, logical analysis, self-control, incorporating change and sound judgement. It is an essential attribute for effective management and helps the manager in decision making and team motivation. People are happy to work for a patient leader and not for those who are impatient and always found standing down their necks.

Guidelines for Improving Patience Levels

Achieving success is no cake walk; it is like keep on rowing the boat persistently and patiently to reach the shores safe and sound. Success is patience and tolerating delays, obstacles and failures. Patience doesn't mean being lethargic, inactive or keep action in abeyance till cows come back home. What I am advocating is be calm and composed and concentrate on your campaign with heart and soul. Some of you may be lucky to have patience as an in-built quality in your personality dynamics. There are others who are impatient and need to practise keeping their minds and emotions calm and stable. Patient people rarely get angry; maintain a good balance between the mind and the heart and are quickly acceptable to people. Developing patience requires some regular practice in day to day life. The following guidelines will be useful:

1. Identify the triggers for impatience

Be aware and sensitive of events and circumstances that usually make you feel anxious, desperate and unhappy. Watch the trend for few days and make a list based on your unbiased assessment of such situations. Next study each of these situations and assess whether these have helped in speeding up the process of execution. Were you able to meet your goals without any hiccups and bumps? How many times have you jumped the gun and realised later that it would have been better to tolerate the delay? What did you miss out? Did you hurt attaining your cherished goal? Identify causes that activate your impatience and plan a suitable response that doesn't disturb your mental equilibrium. It helps to a large extent provided you practise and be patient with the outcome.

2. Remind the self that things take time

Often you may be found whispering, "O God! My patience levels are running out. How soon can I get out of this mess?" It is also common to find most of you hurrying to outplay each other by being impatient all the time. You carry a misnomer that anxiety and being anxious is a ladder to achieving success fast. Just think, has impatience ever paid? On the contrary, it has only impacted your focus and resulted in mental stress, anger and conflicts. Ultimately, you lose on living a productive, esteemed and harmonious life because of negative feelings. Things don't always work the way you plan, it is useful to keep provisions for unexpected delays and happenings. This helps avoid rashness and impatience. There is need to have realistic expectations on the professional front. Steve Ballmer, CEO of Microsoft who replaced Bill Gates at Microsoft, is a leader with passion, patience, and has become a brand of the company. Once he emphasised the importance of patience for succeeding in business, he explained that 'products and businesses go through three phases: vision, patience and execution. 'The patience stage is the toughest and most uncomfortable.' I feel sometimes a crisis situation is an opportunity to self-assess, calm emotions, bring tolerance in your being, learn to change and adjust to the need of the hour. Often you find new ways of managing crisis and a renewed hope of optimism. **Most gratifying things in life take time and dedication and if you're impatient, you're likely to mess up with your success campaign.**

3. Tutoring children

Subject to the availability of time, tutoring children and helping them complete their homework greatly helps in improving patience levels. Most children do all sorts of jugglery to escape studies. One has to live with these excuses by being patient so that the child takes interest in completing his homework. One can also build on patience by testing oneself in small tasks and gradually, shift to bigger tasks.

4. Delegation

Undertaking all the work by yourself and not handing over some part of it to others in the team leads to anger, anxiety and worry which are impatience triggers. Start delegating responsibility among teammates at work. You can coordinate the tasks, provide assistance wherever needed and be accountable. A good housemaker remains patient by delegating jobs to children/maid/other helpers and at times, even to the spouse.

5. Be self-inspired

Patient people do not look for boosting their motivational levels every now and then. They study the situation/ environment and mould their conduct accordingly. This helps them to have good relationship skills and a high acceptance level among people. They believe in mutual cooperation, help and have a positive outlook towards life. Patient people do not interfere in others' issues/tasks unless asked to do so.

6. Improving on listening

Effective listening is an antidote to impatience. People are generally bad listeners and 'old habits die hard.' Patience is of great help in relating effectively with your colleagues, family and friends. Half the problem is resolved if you make the person comfortable, listen patiently and attentively. But often some jump the gun in drawing their own conclusions based more on perception rather than facts. Your mind processes information much faster than the normal rate of speech and you often half-listen, do other things, and think about what next. Discipline the mind to inculcate patience to pay full attention.

7. Managing anger and frustrations

Take a look at this story:-

> *Once a man bought a new truck and next day, he went out to admire it. To his surprise, he found his three-year-old son scratching the shiny paint of the truck. The man ran to his son and hammered his hands as punishment. On calming down, he rushed his son to the hospital. The doctor tried desperately to save the crushed bones; he finally had to amputate the boy's fingers. When the boy woke up from the surgery and saw his hand bandaged, he innocently said, "Daddy, I'm sorry about your truck." Then he asked, "but when are my fingers going to grow back?" The father went home and committed suicide.*

Often when you lose on patience, some of you try to adopt a bull-headed approach in order to impress your own rightness by taking revenge. Making mistakes is no sin, but your response on a rage if not controlled haunts you forever. The art of going beyond anger and frustration lies in learning to let go and flow with the natural unfolding of life.

8. Get out of personality hassles

Impatience is also outcome of your inflated egos. No sooner you get offended, your mind gets into a twister and false ego appears. You do not realise that whatever was communicated reflected the other person's level of thinking and you need not stoop down by being impatient to respond and become angry. Patience is an extraordinary state of mind and you need to control your excitement – both in failure and success.

9. Controlling opinions

Being impatient often affects your judgement and capability to reason and figure out what is right or wrong and you end up making mistakes and hold back your success. Take time to consciously pay attention to your thought process, and then evaluate pros and cons before giving your opinions. Be aware of your feelings to understand your emotional triggers that may commence impatience .Think several times before you speak.

10. Act in response

Before emotionally responding to a situation, evaluate the options you have. This helps to open your mind and chart out the suitable response. Never focus on what others are doing. Be steadfast about working on your own plan. This helps to make your thoughts and actions orderly. Unorganized thoughts and actions usually lead to impatience.

11. Realistic expectations

Remember expectations normally lead to disappointments and impatience. By being realistic and adjusting your expectation levels, you can change the effect on your behaviour and impatience. For example, Disneyland is master at managing waiting by ushering its guests to its theme parks; spend far more time waiting than participating in various activities. Guests are willing to wait longer when they are diverted or entertained. In a way, Disney makes its guests to readjust their expectation levels, be patient by keeping them busy with entertainment. Can you learn readjusting your expectations?

Summing up...

Patience is an upright mind that is able to bear harm and sufferings. It is a state of staying in power, especially during a failure and signifies your elasticity and resolve. Spiritual Guru Sri Chinmoy, once suggested that, **"If failure has the strength to turn your life into bitterness itself, then patience has the strength to turn your life into the sweetest joy."** Learn the art of patience by disciplining thoughts when these become anxious over the outcome of a goal. Patience creates confidence, decisiveness, and a rational outlook, which eventually leads to success. Be mindful and live in the moment.

CHAPTER 26

Meet the Travellers on their Path to Zenith

Following are a selected few individuals from thousands who climbed their path of zenith by visualising accomplishment of their goals and having firm belief in them in spite of facing scores of failures on their mission. They developed a mastermind to architect their success ventures. All of them had a modest beginning, often they did not have bare necessities of life, yet by their unyielding guts and will to perform, they managed to excel in whatever they attempted at. They directed their thoughts, goals and desires and tuned their mind power by focussing on their ultimate mission. They were well aware that there was neither an easy sailing nor a bumpless path to success. Failures on their struggle did not dither them but made them still tough, obstinate and pigheaded. They never hung up their boots but kept fighting and showed great resolve, a great surge to win. Each of their performance was par excellence and in true championship style. They silently pursued their dreams by lighting a candle of hope and ensured survival against the blowing winds. They made mark on success to be like a dark horse and an underdog. As some one said that, **'Success comes in cans', not cants'.**

The stories given briefly below will always remain great inspirations to all those youngsters who want to pin up brand success on their shirts. These are examples of fighting circumstances with all resolutions at command

and recurving a forte for themselves. Stories marked #* are personally known to the author and have been his contemporaries for many years. These great souls did not plan to take this path but when opportunity knocked they seized it. Their stories go to show that you don't have to be 'born with it,' you can develop an unyielding and winning bent of mind.

Take a look:-

- *E Sarathbabu was born and brought up in a slum in Madipakkam, Chennai in India. His mother was the sole breadwinner looking after five children on her meager salary. She sold idlis in the mornings, worked for the mid-day meal at the school during daytime and taught at the Government adult education programme, thus doing three different jobs to bring the family up and educate the children. As a child, Sarathbabu also sold idlis in the slum where he lived. He graduated in Chemical Engineering from BITS, Pilani. He worked for three years in Polaris Software and subsequently went in to pursue his MBA from IIM, Ahmedabad. In December 2006, the Institute's alumni event took place in Mumbai and he decided to go there mainly to get a contract for catering. "I booked my train ticket from Ahmedabad to Mumbai for Rs 300 and I had Rs 200 in my hand. Since the meet went on till late at night, I could reach the station only during the midnight. I missed the train. I decided to sit on the platform till the morning and travel by the next train in the morning. I didn't have the money to check into a hotel. I didn't want to disturb any of my friends so late at night. It was an unforgettable night as I was even shoved off by policemen from the platform. It was quite insulting and embarrassing." Inspired by his mother, who once sold idlis on the pavements of Chennai, Sarathbabu after graduating in Management set-up "Food king" – a food catering services in 2006 with the objective to offer employment to illiterate and semi-illiterate people and improve their standard of living." I put values ahead of money and power. I have learnt it the hard way, rising up from delivering idlis prepared by my mother." "Food*

King" – a food catering business which today employs 300+ people across three centres in India. In 2010, he started "Hunger Free India Foundation" with the objective of contributing in his own way to address the problem of hunger in India through various programmes. *(Excerptes:www.sarathbabu.co.in)*

- *Ed Stafford, a British ex army officer is a great explorer. He has led remote expeditions all over the world and his passion lies in pushing himself to achieve feats that others may not believe are possible. Amazingly no one has ever walked the length of the Amazon river ever and Ed Stafford started his walk in April 2008 from the west coast of Peru on the Pacific coast and completed his walk on 9th August, 2010 and become the real king of jungles. He walked up the deepest canyon in the world to get to the mountain from which the Amazon starts. From the top he knew he had to follow the river for the next two years of his life. Over 4,000 miles lay ahead of him as he started walking - further than the distance to the centre of the Earth. On his great walk through nature's rare secrets, Ed has had to deal with some dangerous things: snakes, jaguars and biting ants all live in the Amazon. Ed was often walking half underwater! In May 2009 Stafford appeared on the cover of the Royal Geographical Society's Geographical magazine.*
- *Pravesh Shrivastava is an embodiment of success, passion, and self- motivation, turning every thing he touches to gold. Coming from a humble and mediocre background, Pravesh initially went to a Hindi medium school. The turning point came when he joined IIT, Roorke, for his graduation in Industrial engineering. A short stint with TELCO, Pune was followed by an MBA from IIM, Kolkatta. "I had no funds but dreams in eyes and pursued studies with education loan and scholarship. My mother used to set goals for me as a student and I have always come up to her expectations." Pravesh made a significant mark when he made it to the Institutes merit list in 1979. Joined Anand Group (sales of about ₹20 crores) in 1979 as an Assistant Manager and today he has turned as a*

professional strength of the Group (sales – ₹4000 crores). Currently Group President HRD & strategy, Chairman Mando India, Chairman Valeo Friction Material, Chairman Faurecia Exhaust Systems, MD Perfect circle India. He is on the board of Takata India and Behr India. Pravesh has the gift of the gab, prudent yet honest, hard working and has an attitude of risk taking. He is an epitome of human relations and a personification for young and aspiring managers.

- *Kal Raman, talented and poor boy from a village in Tirunelveli, Tamil Nadu has risen to be the founder CEO of Global Scholar in Seattle, USA. He lost his father when he was just 15 and his mother got a monthly pension of ₹420($10). The family moved from the rented house to a hut and Raman used to study under the streetlight. He got admission to the Anna University to study Electrical Engineering and Electronics. His first job was with Tata Consulting Engineers, Mumbai and then there was no looking back. On the first day at the job, he went with bag and baggage. The manager noticed that he was wearing slippers to the office. He called him and told him to come to office in shoes. "Only after I get my first pay cheque, can I buy shoes." The manager immediately released a month's salary in advance and also arranged for him to be at his friend's place temporarily. Kal's rise in career was meteoric in a short span of time. Within a month, he got a chance to move to Edinburgh, UK. From Edinburgh, his next stop was the US. In 1992, he went to the US as an entry level with Wal-Mart. When he left Wal-Mart, he was running the information systems for the International Division. Philanthropist Mike Milken convinced Kal to join him and in October 2007, Global Scholar was launched targeting both teachers and students. "I have given jobs to all my friends in the village who were masons and carpenters." He has also adopted all the orphanages around his village.* *(Excerpts: business.rediff.com)*
- *A failure to success story of Geeta Sachdeva is a story of women empowerment. Coming from the interior of Himachal Pradesh and belonging to a highly orthodox*

average background, yet making a name in the corporate world is incredible. Geeta's family was against girls going out for study/work although her mother understood her aspirations. Geeta completed her matriculation followed by a course in shorthand –typing. At the tender age of 18, Geeta started working in a Government Department and side by side pursued her graduation. She subsequently had a stint as a personal secretary with HPMC and Purolator(Anand Group). In spite of being a mother and look after household chores, her strong resolve to continue studies earned her a regular professional diploma in HR. The turning point came in 1984 when she was made training officer and since than there has been no looking back. She was subsequently elevated as Head -HR with Gabriel India Ltd, Parwanoo, HP and then on to Ispat Group as DGM-Organizational Excellence Initiatives followed by Head-HR with a reputed US multinational near Chandigarh. Few years back she became an entrepreneur and has since created a niche in the field of corporate training. She was selected by NPC for a study tour to Japan and Taiwan in the year 1992. "I fought my battles based on conviction. People say I have achieved a lot... but I am still looking for excellence in success which I am sure will come before I hang up my boots."

- *Not many would know of Hemant Topiwalla a matriculate who started his business with Rupees100 (approx US $ 2) to produce and sell Shingar Bindi (cinnabar). Today he owns Shingar Bindi and Tips and Toes Cosmetics in Mumbai and does an annul business of Rupees 5 Corers ($ 1.1 million). He is married to the yesteryear famous TV artist Deepika Chikalia who rose to fame playing Sita in Ramayana and a former Member of Indian Parliament.*
- *Yet another success story is that of Chua Thia Poh, a Chinese now settled in Singapore who left school at the age of16 and made his first million by age 21 by making hooks and spikes for logging industry. It is said that he lost everything by the time he was 25. Gradually, he was able to stabilise and remerge on business scene and founded 'Ho Bee Investment', a property group that developed*

luxury homes in Singapore, China, U.K. This company is believed to have assets more than $1 billion. Chua was just named Businessman of the Year at the Singapore Business Awards, organized by 'The Business Times' and DHL. "My early failure made me even hungrier and determined."

- *Harjinder Kaur who joined Delhi University in early 90's to do a graduation in computer science couldn't speak, understand, and write in English as she had her schooling in Hindi medium in Jind, Haryana. Harjinder was obstinate, worked doubly hard - both at English and her college subjects till she overcame her handicap. With tremendous amount of determination and persistency, she managed to overcome her language handicap by reading her lessons over and over again and consulting dictionaries. "I didn't go for spoken English classes - but I still remember how humiliating it was." Today Harjinder is an expert in computer applications, computer training, and an upcoming entrepreneur and now a CEO of Comvision. She has recently been nominated for the coveted International Women's Entrepreneurial Challenge Award, given jointly by the Manhattan Chamber of Commerce, the Barcelona Chamber of Commerce and FICCI.). A true example of 'what we believe, we can achieve'.* (Excerpts: Mail Today)
- *The story of rags to riches of Patricia Narayan of Mumbai and winner of last year's 'Ficci Woman Entrepreneur of the Year' award is astounding. After a failed marriage in 1982, she started selling eateries from a mobile cart on the Marina beach amidst all odds. After some failed initial attempts, she soon started earning Rs. 600-700($12) and this grew to Rs 25,000 ($500) a day by 2003. She used to personally stand there and sell all the stuff she made and never felt scared to stand even during late nights. She had a sole goal of proving herself. "There was a fire in me that made me believe that I could be successful without anyone's help. I did not want to be a failure. If you have that fire, nothing in the world can stop you from succeeding." But destiny played tyrant with her once again when she lost her daughter and son-in-law*

in a road accident in 2004. It shattered her and for some time she withdrew from her passion. Then her son took over and started the first restaurant 'Sandeepha' in her daughter's memory. It took some time for her to come out of the shock. Today 200 people work for her in her chain of restaurants in Mumbai. From 50 paise a day, her revenue has gone up to ₹2 lakh($4500) a day." Patrica Narayan **advises young entrepreneurs never to lose on self-confidence.** *(Excerpts: business.rediff.com)*

- *Not many would have heard name of Mangte Chungneijang Mary Kom, the 28-year-old brutal boxer and mother-of-two from Manipur, India. She is the only woman boxer to clinch a medal at each of the six World Championships. She has been a five time world champion boxer in 48 Kg. category and created history by winning the World Championship of boxing in Barbados and fifth world boxing champion title in Haikou, China during 2011.Her son recently underwent heart surgery while she was participating in world boxing championship abroad and said that, "Being a world champ boxer means being less of a mum." Mary Kom comes from a poor background and underwent lot of hard work and struggles to reach the zenith of her career. Her sheer staying power is her key to success in spite of discouragements from family who wanted her to spent time on raising her children. She was at times ridiculed and laughed at when she expressed to be a boxing champion.*
- *Dr. Shah Faisal, 27 comes from a remote village of Kashmir (India), studied in a village school, and lost his father in 2002 to militancy. He made history in 2010 by topping the prestigious IAS (Indian Administrative Services) examination in his very first attempt. After the death of his father, his mother took up the reins of helping him fulfill his dream. "I had an exceptional dream, the path was not easy, but I worked hard always visualising being there and I made it without any coaching."*
- *Tejaswini Sawant, a ace shooter from Kolhapur (India) created history in August,2010 when she became the World Champion in the 50m Rifle Prone event in Munich,*

Germany and become the first Indian women to clinch gold at the World Shooting Championship. Tejaswani has been through rough and tough of life on several occasions in the past. She had to procure rifle on installments. Due to the financial constraints she even thought of quitting but for the moral support from her late father.

- *The poorest of poor Abhishek Kumar Bhartiya who scored 154th rank in SC category of IIT-JEE entrance examination 2010 is son of a poor cobbler and would mend shoes in his spare time while his mother stitched old clothes to support the family. Abhishek stayed in a family of six members in one room accommodation having no electricity. He used to prepare for the competition studying under lantern for 5-6 hours without any coaching and tried to pitch in by polishing shoes at his father's shop. But even in the time of happiness, poverty haunts the family. "I am worried about the fees. From where can I manage the amount? This question is troubling my mind."*
- *Dharamveer Kamboj, a matriculate and a poor farmer from Damla village in Haryana was forced out of poverty to come to Delhi to become a rickshaw puller. "I spent about two years as a rickshaw puller. Unfortunately, I met with an accident and had to return to my village." After he got well, he started organic farming in his village, besides a nursery of medicinal plants. There was no way to process the yield into useful products. With his limited resources, he struggled to design and build the first prototype of a cost-effective multipurpose food processing machine. Looking to his innovative capabilities, he has been appointed to the board of Hisar Agricultural University. "When I started my experiments, people used to tease me. They never took me seriously." Remarkable among his farming techniques was the cultivation of mushroom on sugarcane waste. His biggest assets have been positive thinking, hard work and a desire to learn. Today he earns about ₹50,000 ($1000) every month and employees about 25 people. (Excerpts: business.rediff.com)*
- *Coming from the interior of Himachal Pradesh, India, Manohar Tegta had ambitions of pursuing higher studies*

but for his humble background and parental meagre resources, he had to call it a day after graduation. He fondly remembers August 16, 1983 when doors of his destiny opened up with a job on a meagre salary of ₹400 pm ($10). He vividly remembers manager's concluding comments "Young Man, you are destined to go a long way." These words of encouragement have been his back bone of success. "I strongly feel that to have a 'Role Model' very early in one's career helps in a big way. Initial nurturing, hand holding and guidance helped me to travel a significant distance." With his persistency, hard work, and keeping head above the water, Manohar has steadily risen in life. Today he is G M – HR with Godrej Consumer Products for their Himachal Pradesh manufacturing plants in India. In addition, he oversees HR operations of Godrej manufacturing locations in Sarac countries. Earlier he had stints with reputed organisations like Purolator India, Remington Rand., Avery India, Unichem and Piramal Healthcare. He says "I am on a mission and Journey still continues"...............

- *Coming from an average family background, VVS Mani started doing CA article ship along with his Graduation. But some where down the line, he had to drop his CA exams because he had to contribute to the family income. So he took up a sales job with Yellow Pages in 1987. From 1992 to 1996, he worked on different ideas to survive and to save some money to start Just Dial. This included a concept called Wedding Planner, which was in tie-up with The Times of India. In 1989, he started a company called Ask Me Service. "Those were the days when people had to wait years to get phone connections. The idea was good and well-appreciated, but we didn't see any financial gains from it." He subsequently wound up it and landed up in Mumbai in 1996 with a sum of ₹50,000 to find a home and an office space. Both weren't easy to find. Mani soon succeeded in renting a 25-square feet office in Mumbai's Nariman Point for ₹5000 a month. In those days, a phone line used to cost ₹15,000 under OYT or else one had to wait for few years. He did not have ₹15,000 for a phone. He applied by paying ₹3000 and actually the phone came a year later! Finally, he started Just Dial, with some borrowed furniture, rented PCs and with a capital of ₹50,000! Mani today has built a business with an annual turnover of ₹100 crores and a valuation in excess of ₹500 crores, a database of 2 million business records and 10 million regular users. Just Dial receives on an average more than three million enquiries per month along with having 2700 employees across 12 Indian cities. He has taken his phone-based business model to print, online and SMS. He is now busy executing an International rollout. (Excerpts: kamyabology.com)*

- *Ben Saunders, a British polar explorer, endurance athlete and motivational speaker was plump and shy at school and the last kid in his class picked for any sports team possibly he was considered useless. He was supposed to be an object of jokes and ridiculed in school gym classes in England's rural Devon County. Gradually, Saunders set his mind on building up his body, increasing his speed, strength and endurance. At age 18, he ran his first marathon. There was no looking back once he got in to Royal Military Academy, Sandhurst. In 2001, after becoming a proficient skier, Saunders embarked on his first long-distance expedition toward the North Pole. It took incredible stamina. He suffered frostbite, had a close encounter with a polar bear. He is best known for skiing solo to the North Pole in 2004, and for being the third in history and the youngest by ten years to reach the North Pole alone and on foot. He holds the record for the longest solo Arctic journey by a Briton, a straight line distance of 1032.3 km. Once he said, "I am an explorer of limits – geographically, physically and mentally. It's about pure human endeavour, and the way in which I can inspire others to explore their own personal potential." (Excerpts: Readers Digest, July, 2005).*
- *Prem Ganapathy from Tuticorin, India left home without informing his parents in pursuit of making money at age 17. In 1990, he found a job as a dishwasher in one of the bakeries and worked for about two years*

across restaurants in Mumbai doing odd jobs. Realising that there was good potential in the catering business, he took a handcart on rent to sell idli, dosa and vada in 1992. His items became run away success as these had different flavor and variety. Five years later, Ganapathy was confident enough to open the first Prem Sagar Dosa Plaza outlet outside Vashi station in Navi Mumbai. Since then there has been no looking back. Dosa Plaza has indeed become a runaway success. Today, he has 35 outlets including franchisees with a turnover of over ₹5 crores ($1.1million). In 2008, he opened franchisee outlets in New Zealand and has plans to open outlets in the US and Dubai. In 2010 he opened third outlet in New Zealand. The Dosa Plaza success story has also become a case study for management students.

- *Naresh Gulati of Chandigarh, India, a self-made millionaire with revenues of over Aus$ 19 million (₹80 crores)* ***is a finest example of failure turned to success.*** *He was labelled as a failure by his family and relatives for he spent time selling candles and cloth in the streets of Chandigarh and was novice in speaking English and even failed in his 10th class examination. In spite of his lack of interest in studies, he was forced to complete his graduation by his parents. Subsequently he did a course in electronic data processing. He was even duped by dishonest travel agents who promised him a lucrative career in Australia. Everyone thought he had ruined his life but he never thought he was a failure. He did what he thought he was good at: business. So what if it meant selling candles or cloth on the streets? After the post-graduate course in information systems from RMIT University, Melbourne, he got a job as an analyst programmer. During his studies he used to do part time work at times even washing dishes. But this did not lessen his resolve to succeed. He worked for one year and came back to India in 1996 and set up Oceanic Consultants Australia (OCA), a Melbourne-based company that has three subsidiaries that offer a range of services to the international education industry. The Group comprises of three businesses: Oceanic*

Consultants, BPO Intelligence and Object Next Software. (Excerpts: business.rediff.com)

- *Allex Miller graduated in 2009, but couldn't land a job and found himself with a sense of impending failure. Days felt like weeks, weeks like months and the most frustrating part was no matter how much he tried, he just couldn't seem to make any progress. So what did he do to maintain his sanity? He started writing. Something about putting words on a page made everything seem a little clearer - a little brighter. Something about writing gave him hope. He channeled his frustration into a children's book- "Beyond the River", the story of an unlikely hero featuring a little fish who simply refused to give up on his dream. Two years later, his life has done a complete 180 degrees turn about. He is now working for The Walt Disney Company after having landed subsequent publishing contracts for works he wrote while homeless. "I just wanted to let people know that there is light at the end of the tunnel. (Abridged: Alex W. Miller.motivateus.com)*
- *After finishing her bachelor's degree in chemical engineering from Chandigarh, Ms. Ovessa Iqbal, 25 years old hailing from remote Chachoot village in Ladakh region, is among the seven successful candidates from J&K state to have cracked the UPSC examination in 2011 and the first Muslim woman from the state to make it the prestigious civil services list. Iqbal failed to even get past the preliminary round in her first attempt in 2008. She worked hard and got through to the mains the next year but could not cross the final hurdle. In the meantime, she appeared in Kashmir Administrative Service (KAS) examination in 2010 and qualified. However, she did not rest on her laurels and appeared at the national level again in 2010. "The credit for my success goes to my family as without their efforts it would not have been possible for me to crack the examination," said Iqbal. (Excerpts: asianage.com/India)*

Just Think!

Success, happiness and satisfaction are made for each other and remain true only if these go together, complement and enhance each other. When that happens, you'll experience an exultant joy like never before and conclude a part of your journey to the zenith when you bask in the glow of the flash bulbs and adoring with flowers and garlands all over. What kind of heritage you build and leave behind brings success and immense joy incomparable to big bank balances and physical assets. Have you ever thought that there are a whole lot of magnitudes to life which are of greater value and need fulfilling before you call quits to your life journey? The push for rushing forward has to come from within. Unless you create that push, life will remain unexciting and going through a motion of repeated failures and setbacks.